THE POWER OF PUBLIC SPEAKING

by Marie Stuttard

BARRON'S

First U.S. edition published in 1997 by Barron's Educational Series, Inc.

First published in 1995 by
David Bateman Limited
Tarndale Grove
Albany Business Park
Bush Road, Albany
AUCKLAND 1330
NEW ZEALAND

All inquiries should be addressed to:
Barron's Educational Series, Inc.
250 Wireless Boulevard
Hauppauge, New York 11788

Library of Congress Catalog Card No. 96-32955

International Standard Book No. 0-8120-9794-7

Library of Congress Cataloging-in-Publication Data
Stuttard, Marie.
    The power of public speaking / by Marie Stuttard.
        p.   cm.
    ISBN 0-8120-9794-7
    1. Public speaking.   I. Title
PN4121.S8345   1996
808.5'1—dc20   96-32955
                                         CIP

Cover and book design by Marquerite van Bergen, Charisma Digital

Printed in Hong Kong
987654321

To my darling daughter, Elizabeth

CONTENTS

PREFACE

The Power of Public Speaking is a companion volume to *The Power of Speech* (Barron's 1996). They are meant to be studied together. *The Power of Speech* concentrates on language, the voice, and presentation. Subjects include how to overcome nerves, gain confidence, become a fluent speaker, and sound like a professional.

The Power of Public Speaking leads you onto a platform to make a speech. No one can tell you exactly what to say, but I have tried to give you an awareness of what audiences expect, and how you can fulfill those expectations in a fluent, stimulating, and memorable way.

Speaking in public is high on the list of most people's worst fears. This book is designed to take away that fear and help you discover the methods used by successful and experienced speakers.

As in *The Power of Speech*, there are no chapters. Every two pages are complete in themselves, so that you can open it anywhere and learn.

There is information on a wide variety of subjects, from researching your topic to making an impression in the first 60 seconds—and beyond. The moon chart—an amazingly simple way to prepare material for speaking in public—has been borrowed from *The Power of Speech* because it just has to be here!

Everything I write is the result of a lifetime's experience. I hold a teacher's diploma from the Guildhall School of Speech and Drama, London, and have been broadcasting on radio and television with the B.B.C. and in New Zealand for many years. I am a corporate lecturer in speech and communication.

My passion for language also includes the written word. This is my tenth book, but I have been a journalist for a morning newspaper, a writer for a weekly magazine, as well as a *Vogue* fashion editor.

I would like you to look upon speaking in public as a challenge. When you have learned how to express your thoughts and ideas, pass on your knowledge and inspire an audience, you will find that your life will change. Success breeds not only success but confidence, and that confidence will open up a whole new world for you.

Don't let anything stop you. Once you can stand up and say even a few words in public, you've made the breakthrough. Keep at it. Listen and learn, but develop your own highly individual style.

Marie Stuttard

WHAT

IS

A

SPEECH ?

A GOOD QUESTION

The word *speech* covers a wide variety of activities. From the simple "thank you" it can grow bigger and more important as it goes from talk to sermon, from lecture to oration. Each type of speech is designed to appeal to a specific group, but obviously what all speeches have in common is that they are delivered before an audience. The audience can vary in size from a few to a hundred, to a thousand or more.

FEAR OF FOLKS

What is accepted throughout the world is that standing up before an audience of any size is one of the most frightening acts a human can perform.

What is it that makes us so terrified of making a speech in public? Is it the audience? Or is it a fear deep within ourselves? It is probably a blend of the two. Many public speakers regard an audience as a mass of monsters, ready to tear them apart, yet they are just ordinary folks like ourselves. Ask any of them to stand up and speak out and most of them would hide.

THE TARGET

Collectively people can be somewhat intimidating, but only if we let them. The secret is not to let them. Always regard an audience as a group of individuals; people like ourselves with hopes and desires, fears and phobias. This doesn't mean we should ignore them and speak only to please ourselves. On the contrary, every word we utter should be directed at our target—our audience—giving them information, inspiration, enjoyment, or whatever is the purpose of the speech.

THE FIRST APPROACH

APPRECIATE

THE COMPLIMENT

BUT BE

CAUTIOUS

MORE THAN MEETS THE EYE

When someone invites you to speak at a conference or any social event, the tendency is to say "Yes, thank you."

But before you accept any speaking engagement there is much to find out. It is easier if you already know about the organization and what they'll want. If you don't, then it is imperative that you find out. Ask who they are, what they do, why they want you, and how they found you.

FACTS AND FEE

Get as much information as you can before you make a decision. Find out where you will have to go, what they expect from you, and the fee they are offering. You also need to know how you fit in with their overall program, how long your speech should be, who the other speakers are, and in which order they will be speaking.

If the engagement is not in your own town or city, you have to find out where you will stay and inform them how long beforehand you wish to arrive. Some speakers like to get there the day before. If the event is in another country, that time would probably be two days to let you overcome time changes. Nothing dampens a speech like a tired speaker.

"YES"...BUT

You have to have enough information to judge whether the engagement is right for you. Check your calendar to make sure that nothing on it conflicts with the date. This is especially important if the engagement is out of town.

Once you say "yes," there are still a few points to consider. Make sure they spell your name correctly on the program. Make sure, too, that the title of your speech and the information they put in the program about you are accurate.

GETTING DOWN TO THE

Nitty Gritty

YOU HAVE BEEN ASKED TO SPEAK

AND

YOU HAVE ACCEPTED

WHAT DO YOU DO NEXT?

AT THE BEGINNING

Once a date has been agreed upon you have to start organizing immediately. Selecting the right topic is vital. You have to decide on a subject your audience will relate to, so think of one from their perspective rather than yours. Consider their lifestyle and look for a hook that will appeal to them.

You must have an overall plan. Ask yourself what the main point is that you want to get across. When this is resolved you will have the skeleton of your speech.

DRESSING THE BONES

To give life to your speech you need a message that comes from the heart. It must be what you believe in, have a passion for, and wish to offer to your audience. Without it, your speech will be flat and uninteresting.

However, emotion without reason is seldom acceptable, so, use your head, your brain, your intellect. Work out your plot to include other aspects of your main theme. Expand it so that you include details, references, anecdotes, and humor.

FASHIONABLE FRAME

Your speech now should have all the elements needed to hold and satisfy your audience. When what began as mere bones becomes a living being, you can start thinking about how it is to be presented. Is it going to be a dramatic speech or an intimate one? Will you be supplying factual information and need some form of visuals? Do you plan to introduce material that requires a lot of research?

Take time to prepare your basic plan. It will pay off later.

HOW

TO

INVOLVE

YOUR

AUDIENCE

ASK—DON'T ASSUME

To "win" at your speaking engagement, you need to begin work as soon as you receive your booking. To simply write it down on your calendar is not enough. By the time you actually get there and face your audience, you could be speaking to them on a subject or at a level that is not entirely suitable.

GIVE ME A CLUE

Ask questions. Apart from finding out where you will give your speech, the time you're expected to arrive and so on, find out the type and the age of audience you'll be speaking to.

The organization that invited you may give you a clue. It could be the Salvation Army, a city council, or an annual dinner for a large corporation. But again, knowing that is not enough.

You need to know approximately how many will be attending to determine whether it is to be a speech on a grand scale or a cozy, more informal one.

THE RATIO

Find out the economic background of your audience. This will give you a chance to gear your speech to their needs. The educational background of the audience can also help you to deliver an appropriate speech.

Discover the possible ratio of men to women. This information can play an important role in the form of speech you give—not to mention the references you may make while giving it. The possible ethnic ratio is helpful too. For instance, you may have information that could be valuable to new immigrants.

But if you don't ASK you won't know. Don't assume anything.

RESEARCH

Doing what
you have
to do

YOUR PART OF THE BARGAIN

When you're invited to give a speech you enter into a bargain. What you say must be credible and reliable. If, through carelessness, you renege on your contract, you are the loser. You may not be trusted in the future.

So, like it or not, if you are giving more than just your opinions, if you include statistics or any material that requires verifying, you must research your information thoroughly.

HELP!

First of all decide what you actually do know for sure. It is surprising how much information you can have stacked away in your head or in reference books at home. Decide which areas need extra information and get to work.

You may be able to do some of it by telephone. A call to a friend or business associate might result in getting what you want. If not, a visit to a library gives you the opportunity to study a vast amount of information through reference books, books of quotations and statistics, different forms of encyclopedias, and books on almost every subject you may need. If in doubt, ask the librarian for help. You may need to go elsewhere for details or data, but always make sure your sources are reliable.

EDITING

There can be a danger in having too much information. After a lot of research you could be left with a frightening amount of it. You can't use it all. You only need some of it, so carefully edit out what you feel will make your speech dull or top heavy. Make sure, too, that what you do retain is relevant to your audience.

KNOW

YOUR

AUDIENCE

WHO ARE YOU SPEAKING TO?

We can't know the likes and dislikes of every member of an audience, but there are ways of finding out some basic guidelines. These guidelines help you to plan your speech, include relevant information, and also present your speech.

If you're going into an obviously favorable environment, you have the knowledge that your topic will be well received. This allows you to spice it up with anecdotes and perhaps stories about people known to you all.

ERROR-FREE

If, however, you suspect that your audience could be somewhat hostile to you and your arguments, then everything you say must be thoroughly researched and accurately presented. You cannot allow any member of that audience to pierce your reasoning easily. Make sure facts and figures are correct and all information is as error-free as possible. Rather than being one-sided with such an audience, it pays to include both sides of an argument so they realize that you are at least aware of them.

BE YOURSELF

Sometimes you may be invited to speak in front of an audience that is a little above or below your level of education. Don't be intimidated or talk down. You're there because you have something of interest to tell them. Be yourself. Be natural and persuasive, and no matter who is there, how many or how few, give your best.

It is inspiring to see top speakers put as much effort into speaking to a handful of underprivileged people as they would when addressing a group of the so-called elite.

Wordpower

is to the mind

what horsepower

is to a

car.

EDWARD DE BONO
WORDPOWER

UP AND RUNNING

If you want to be a successful public speaker you won't get far without "word power." Even if you write your speech out in detail, you still need word power to prepare it.

Word power comes into its own when you step onto a platform. Language must have meaning and depth. Language must be rich in imagery. Language must be so potent that every person in your audience is affected by it.

PUT THEM TOGETHER

Word power doesn't just mean selecting individual words. It is how you put them together that really stamps you as a professional. It is the flair you inject into them as sentences, paragraphs, and complete messages. Some people have the ability to take a few ordinary little words and create magic with them.

After a seminar once, people came up and said, "Thank you. I enjoyed it very much." But one person said, "Marie, I am weeping tears of joy because today you showed me a world I never knew existed." I was bowled over.

ABSORBED

Word power can't be "learned" in the accepted sense, but it can be absorbed by constantly listening, reading widely, and thinking up your own ways of expressing yourself.

Make yourself aware of how you can expand your word power. Talk to yourself out loud. Talk about a vacation, a meeting, a scene, an event. Describe them, add emotions and color. Change to intimate revelations then dramatic experiences. Phrase and rephrase. Talk, talk, talk.

The Draaft

from

INITIAL JUGGLING WITH

THOUGHTS AND IDEAS

to

THE FINAL VERSION

PUTTING IT ON PAPER

Whether you write by hand, on a typewriter, or on a computer, try getting those first thoughts down on paper. Get over the fear of not knowing what to say—allow the words to tumble from your mind. Let your imagination roll. It doesn't matter if your ideas come out as a jumble. You are at least creating images. You can tidy them up—or eliminate many of them—later. The main thing is to get started.

BE FANCIFUL

As any writer will tell you, the toughest job is looking at a blank piece of paper, so just do it. Be fanciful. Be instructive. Add color and character, and think up suitable anecdotes. Remember a funny story or two. But get it down in words.

Step two is editing what you have written. It is surprising how you can look at what's there and suddenly get a totally different approach to your subject. If you do, then start again.

If you're happy with what you've got, prune it or expand it according to your needs.

READ ALOUD

As you move further into your draft make sure that your speech has a bright opening, a strong middle, and a satisfying ending. As you go, keep the ideas flowing. Sometimes one good idea can lead you to make changes in direction or at least the flavor of what you want to say.

Keep reading your draft aloud. This allows you to discover where information is disjointed. It gives you the opportunity to fill out or weed out before you actually deliver your speech and it reveals whether or not you are hopping from one subject to another.

IF

language is not correct, then what is said is not what is meant; if what is said is not what is meant, then what ought to be done remains undone.

CONFUCIUS

OUT WITH NONSENSE

Isn't it incredible that advice like this was handed to us in the fifth century B.C., and we still haven't learned a lot from it? Do you listen to people in power, in politics, to those who hold administrative positions and wonder how some of them got there? The nonsense, the wordiness, the twaddle, the blather, the aimless and often misleading verbosity makes what they say difficult to understand.

Make sure you avoid these pitfalls.

CLEAR AND LOGICAL

Fine tune your thinking. Learn to edit your language just as a newspaper editor does with the written word. Cut out unnecessary talk for talk's sake. Have a clear picture in your mind of what you want to say. Color it with relevant material. But what you do say must come out in a logical way with one idea following the other so that the whole makes perfect sense.

Your audience may not like what you say. They may disagree with your argument. They may even become a little hostile, but at least they'll know exactly what you mean.

ONE WORD

You must be careful too that the actual words you choose have the exact meaning you want to get across. Occasionally I have heard speakers use words that obviously do not fit in with what they're saying.

Language is very subtle. There are shades of meaning. I'm constantly checking my dictionary to make sure I've got the word I need. If it turns out not to be just what I want, I go to a thesaurus to find one that is.

THE THREE WISE MONKEYS

(MARIE'S VERSION)

SEEING   HEARING   FEELING

FEEDING THE BRAIN

If you want to leave a lasting impression on an audience you can program them just as you would a computer. It is all very well to tell people to "do this" or "do that," but much of what you say may have disappeared from their memories by the time they leave the hall.

People retain information in three basic ways: through the eyes (visuals), the ears (auditory), and through feelings (kinesthetics). Each of us usually favors one more than the others. I remember better when I see a name or information written down.

DIFFERENT GROUPS

By including references to each of these categories in your speech you are actually appealing to the different groups. For instance, the visual people like phrases that include words such as *see, look,* and *watch.* The audiophiles among us respond to *listen, hear,* and *sound,* while the kinesthetics go for *touch, taste, feel,* and *smell.*

Have you ever been won over by expert salespeople? Without you even being aware of it, they could have been reflecting the type of language you use so that you feel comfortable with them. It is possible also to mirror another's body language and movements—crossing your legs, folding your arms, and so on.

WORTH STUDYING

Neuro Linguistic Programming (NLP) is the study of perception and behavior that gives you a greater awareness of verbal and nonverbal communication skills. It is a complex subject but one that is well worth studying with an expert.

ONCE UPON A TIME...

DISCOVER
THE
STORYTELLER

IN YOURSELF

COME CLOSER—AND LISTEN!

The power of the storyteller is enormous. Audiences love stories. They learn from them, and well-told stories help listeners to remember the information they hear.

Brilliant raconteurs cast spells over their audiences and they are always in demand. You may not be in that category, but if you can tell a story with a little flair you'll find that it will do wonders for your ability as a speaker.

START SMALL

To test this ability try making up a story and telling it to children. Keep your story simple and easy to follow. Add dialogue from a range of characters. Throw in some colorful descriptions, suspense, danger, drama.

Observe their reaction. Are they interested? Is your delivery exciting enough to hold their attention? Can you make them laugh? Can you make them feel sad? Can you involve them so much in your story that they want more? At what point do they start shuffling or moving away?

GO WITH THE FLOW

You can learn a lot about yourself from encounters like this. With children, you can let yourself go in a way you may not have the courage to do with adults— especially those you don't know. Yet once you get into the flow of storytelling, you may be amazed at how well you do it.

Practice makes each storytelling a little bit better. You learn how to hold your audiences and how to inject relevant stories into even serious speeches. If you plan to include one in a speech, rehearse it, over and over again, until you feel really happy with it.

PREPARING YOUR SPEECH

IN THE FORM OF A

SCRIPT

MANUSCRIPT

TEXT

MANUAL

HANDBOOK

PAPER

DOCUMENT

SO YOU CAN READ IT

EASILY

PREVENT THE PANIC

Before you even begin to think about what you will write down, it is important to work out the method you'll use. Whether it will be handwritten, prepared on a typewriter, or on a computer on one side only, you will need to be able to read it at a greater distance than usual.

For this reason it has to be very easy to read, especially as you will be lifting your head and looking at your audience throughout your speech. I've seen many people completely thrown by not finding the right place when they look down again.

THE GRIP

Inexperienced speakers often prepare their speeches on thin, slippery paper, then regret that choice. It creases, is difficult to separate, and sometimes flutters to the ground. You need a reasonably thick, quality paper. Rather than turning the pages over, it is simpler to turn up a corner of each page then slide it away to the other side of the lectern. This has the advantage of the audience not being so aware that you are actually reading your speech.

SEE-ALL TYPE

Handwriting must be large, and it is imperative that the typed or printed letters are big enough for you to read every word without straining. You can use capital letters throughout if you find it easier. Triple spacing is best; anything smaller is risky. A double triple between paragraphs makes each one stand out, and every page should have wide margins at each side.

A simple-to-read script can be left on the lectern while you use the platform as an actor would. You can walk about, use more body language, and still be able to read from it when necessary.

LAYOUTS FOR MANUSCRIPTS

XXXXXXXXXXXX
XXXXXXXXXXXX
XXXXXXXXXXXX

    XXXXXXXXXXXX
    XXXXXXXXXXXX
    XXXXXXXXXXXX

XXXXXXXXXXXX
XXXXXXXXXXXX
XXXXXXXXXXXX

A   XXXXXXXXXXXX
    XXXXXXXXXXXX
    XXXXXXXXXXXX

B   XXXXXXXXXXXX
    XXXXXXXXXXXX
    XXXXXXXXXXXX

C   XXXXXXXXXXXX
    XXXXXXXXXXXX
    XXXXXXXXXXXX

1   XXXXXXXXXXXX
XXXXXXXXXXXX
2   XXXXXXXXXXXX

A   XXXXXXXXXXXX
  1 XXXXXXXXXXXX
  2 XXXXXXXXXXXX
  3 XXXXXXXXXXXX

B   XXXXXXXXXXXX
  1 XXXXXXXXXXXX
  2 XXXXXXXXXXXX

C   XXXXXXXXXXXX
  1 XXXXXXXXXXXX
  2 XXXXXXXXXXXX

THE BASICS

You can see that by arranging your paragraphs in quick-to-pick-up ways, you save yourself from continually having to wonder where you should read from next. It is also a good idea to mark each paragraph boldly with different letters or numbers, preferably with colored markers.

Never run a paragraph over to the next page. This can be most confusing. It makes you hesitate while you find your place and affects your voice and the conviction you're trying to put into it.

THE NUMBERS GAME

Number every page. This is essential. If, by chance, you drop your speech or the pages get mixed when you pull them out of your briefcase, you must be able to sort them out immediately. The top right-hand corner of a page is best for numbering.

Don't staple the pages together. You need to be able to handle them without your audience being distracted as you flip over one page after another.

Some people have just two paragraphs on each page, triple spaced, with a line drawn across the middle. It is very simple to read.

FLYAWAY

A lot of speakers use small handheld notes. These are all right, but they look amateurish. If you do use them, select a heavy paper, index cards, or even light cardboard. Flyaway paper is difficult to control.

It is advisable to make at least two copies of your speech—one for yourself on which you can record all your personal messages about delivery; the other either for your records or adapted to be read and handed to the press (see pages 148–149).

DISCOVER THE BENEFITS OF MARKING YOUR SCRIPT

Underline the words you want to

EMPHASIZE

Use a vertical line / to denote a pause

This symbol ∧ tells you when the voice

should rise and fall on one word

BRING YOUR SPEECH TO LIFE

These three simple symbols can help you transform your speech from just words into words with purpose, meaning, and expression. They not only give you a visual message of how to say your speech but remind you how to fine tune your language, so that it always comes across effectively and with style.

The first time you read your speech out loud it may sound a little flat and un-interesting, so put the symbols in to bring out the meaning and give it greater vitality.

A LITTLE JERKY?

Read it aloud again. This time it may sound somewhat jerky, but read it aloud again and again until the pauses are what I call "flowing" pauses. You'll discover then that your speech comes to life in a smooth and vital way. The more you read aloud, the easier it is to get used to listening to the sound of your own voice.

READ THIS PARAGRAPH ALOUD

"Unfortunately many people still use written-style language in speech, yet the two are different. While the written word is grammatical, structured, and more formal, the spoken word should be easy, less structured, but fluent and eloquent."

NOW PUT THE SYMBOLS IN

"Unfortunately / many people / still use / written style language / in speech, / yet / the two / are different. / While the written word / is / grammatical, / structured / and more formal, / the spoken word / should be / easy, / less structured / but fluent / and eloquent."

T H O U G H T S

ABOUT

PREPARATION

FOR THE

BIG DAY

FIRST THINGS FIRST

Don't wait until the last minute to decide what you are going to wear when you have to make a speech. Plan early, for you may have to buy something new. Certainly study what you have in your wardrobe first, but sometimes you take out a favorite outfit and—horror!—discover you've put on weight and it doesn't fit properly, or it looks more worn or dated than you remembered.

COORDINATED

It is most important that you feel comfortable in your "platform" clothes. Choose suitable clothes and accessories to go with them. The coordinated look is vital when appearing in public. A bit of this and a bit of that and your audience might think your brain is that way too.

Be particularly careful with color. The color you wear can make a tremendous difference in your overall look, especially if the platform is brightly lit. It's a good investment to have your colors done professionally. You need to know which colors enhance you and which drain you. This applies to men as well as to women.

DRESS FOR SUCCESS

It is always advisable to buy the best clothes you can afford. A good cut, fine fabric, and a suitably colored garment make you feel like a million dollars. A badly fitting one does the opposite.

To keep your confidence high you literally have to dress for success. If you can't afford a lot, browse around some good quality secondhand shops. Many a wonderful bargain has been picked up there.

WHEN YOU WALK ONTO A PLATFORM

THE

FIRST THING

PEOPLE

NOTICE

ABOUT

YOU

IS YOUR

APPEARANCE

LOOKING THE PART

That first glance creates an image. Afterwards your audience couldn't itemize what you wore, but they certainly could say that you seemed dated or fashionable, scruffy or immaculate, tasteless or sophisticated.

It may not only be you they're judging, but your company, your club, or your organization. You owe it to yourself—and to those you may represent—to present a picture that is both appealing and professional.

TOP TO TOE

The leading ingredient of image is, of course, good grooming. The essential cleanliness and polish goes from your styled hair to the toes of your shining shoes. Poor grooming puts people off. That first look may take in the uncreased dress, skirt, or pants, or the spotless shirt or blouse.

The style of your clothes is also important. A woman, for instance, can seem old fashioned if her skirt is too long. If she looks old fashioned, the audience may assume that her information is out-of-date too. A skirt that is only hip length may give the impression of a bimbo with limited intelligence. And jewelry should not be so eye catching or jangly that it is distracting.

ONE EXTREME TO THE OTHER

If a man's suit is from another era—even if it is only a few years before—it can make him appear passé in more ways than one. If a speaker hasn't a suitable suit in his wardrobe, I suggest renting one for the occasion. Ties range from ultra-conservative and attractive to downright garish. Because they're so visible, they too can have an impact on an audience.

We may laugh at these generalizations, but frequently you hear people summing up speakers because of the way they look. So it pays to examine yourself critically before you set foot on a platform.

THOSE

PERSONAL

PRELIMINARIES

IT PAYS TO PREPARE

No matter how carefully you prepare, last-minute hitches can occur. Some details are seemingly so unimportant that you don't even think about them beforehand—and I'm not talking about visuals and so on. Rather it is the little things that may cause problems or make you appear uncomfortable.

As soon as possible find out where the rest room (lavatory, toilet) is. This may sound trivial, but believe me, it is vital. If you need to go at the last minute and can't, it will cause surprising stress.

ALL CLEAN AND CORRECT

If your dress or suit creases when traveling or sitting, it pays to carry it with you and put it on just before you speak.

Check your teeth, especially if you have a meal at the affair. Nothing puts an audience off more than to see a bit of food stuck between a speaker's front teeth, and nothing is more embarrassing for you than to discover it afterwards. Have a mini toothbrush in your pocket and use it.

CHECK AND DOUBLE CHECK

If you comb your hair before going onto the platform, make sure that you haven't left stray hairs on your shoulders—or worse—dandruff. It is a good idea to carry a mirror with you as not all rest rooms have them. Even if there is one, your little mirror allows you to see yourself from the back and sides as well.

If you've walked up a muddy path to get to the place, take a moment to clean your shoes and check that your panty hose or trousers are not splattered.

WHAT SHOULD YOU DO

IF

You go to the wrong place?

You're held up and arrive late?

You leave a page of your notes at home?

MESSING THINGS UP

These things do happen; and when they do they can make the next hour or so miserable for you.

You can arrive at the wrong place if you don't make absolutely sure you know where it is. Sometimes we assume we know these things. Sometimes the organizers assume we know. *Don't* make assumptions. Get a detailed description of where the place is, how to get there, and, if you have any doubts, ask for a map with the place marked on it, even if it is drawn by hand. When you leave home, don't forget to take the instructions with you.

TARDY—AND TRAUMATIZED

Being held up and arriving late can happen to anyone. It only takes an accident or bad weather to delay or even cancel your arrival. This creates the most dreadful feeling of letting people down. If possible, have a contact telephone number for the place where you are to speak or for someone who could relay a message. If there is any danger of your being late, telephone ahead, even if you have to get out of your car in a snowstorm to do so. When you do arrive, make your apologies then give it your best.

The only time being late is inexcusable is if you are the culprit and haven't organized your time properly.

NAUGHTY! NAUGHTY!

There is absolutely no excuse for leaving a page of your speech behind. The last thing you should do before leaving is CHECK every page, every visual, every item you want to bring with you—and have an extra copy of your speech with you as well.

TIMING

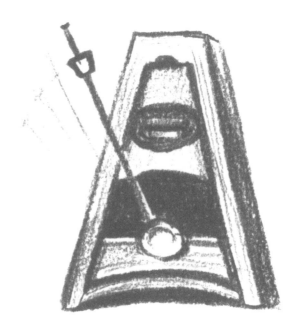

AND ALL THAT JAZZ

CONFIDENCE AT ITS BEST

Timing could be described as "pause plus." Whereas the pause adds the professional touch to speech, timing affects speakers from the moment they arrive at their engagement until they leave. Have you ever noticed how some inexperienced people behave? I call it gabbling: they stumble or stutter, obviously nervous, hurry onto a platform and rush through their speeches, then collapse with relief afterwards.

Those who have a sense of timing make everything look effortless. You can see it even in the way they greet their hosts, wait to speak, and face their audiences.

NOT PANIC

I've seen some speakers look at their audiences for a surprisingly long time before they launch into their topic. Listeners wait, intrigued. There is a feeling of anticipation. This isn't a case of lost words or panic. It is sheer professionalism. Listeners can sense confidence without a word being spoken.

Then they do speak. Through their timing, as well as what they say, experienced speakers can hold their audiences for as long as they wish, just as great jazz singers use timing superbly as they manipulate music to express their feelings and enchant their audiences.

SECOND NATURE

You can't learn timing. You develop it. You get so aware of it that it becomes second nature to incorporate it into everything you do. Study people; watch them, listen to them. Discover how they can turn ordinary occasions into something special by their use of timing.

THE OTHER SIDE

TICK... TICK... TICK... TICK...

TICK... TICK... TICK... TICK... TICK... TICK... TICK... TICK...

TICK... TICK... TICK... TICK... TICK... TICK... TICK... TICK...

TICK... TICK... TICK... TICK... TICK... TICK... TICK... TICK...

TICK... TICK... TICK... TICK... TICK... TICK... TICK... TICK...

TICK... TICK... TICK... TICK... TICK... TICK... TICK... TICK...

TICK... TICK... TICK... TICK... TICK... TICK... TICK... TICK...

TICK... TICK... TICK... TICK... TICK... TICK... TICK... TICK...

TICK... TICK... TICK... TICK... TICK... TICK... TICK... TICK...

TICK... TICK... TICK... TICK... TICK... TICK... TICK... TICK...

TICK... TICK... TICK... TICK... TICK... TICK... TICK... TICK...

TICK... TICK... TICK... TICK... TICK... TICK... TICK... TICK...

TICK... TICK... TICK... TICK... # OF TIMING

TICKTOCK TIMING

There is another interpretation of the word *timing*. It is more practical and every bit as important to a public speaker as the one that injects professionalism into a speech. This timing is connected with the clock.

It is imperative that a sense of timing is involved in every move you make. You must plan how long it will take you to get to your destination, allowing for unexpected delays or accidents. You must be aware of the time it will take you to check the room or hall, discover where you will speak, what facilities are available, and how they work.

THE EARLY BIRD

You may be able to find out beforehand what kind of microphone you will be using. This is good but you need to be in early to examine it. The same applies to equipment such as visuals, screens, projector stands, and even to extension cords and lighting. The time factor is vital.

You have to allow time for a final trip to the rest room, perhaps a change of dress or suit. Certainly freshening up will be needed before you appear on the platform.

CLOCKWORK

Your speech has to be timed with reasonable accuracy. If you go on too long— or finish too early—you can throw the organization of the whole event out of kilter. I've seen promoters almost panic-stricken when this happens. Question and answer time also has to be kept within a tight framework. If people in the audience prattle on, you must have the confidence and the authority to rein them in. Every second counts.

No

No!

TO NEGATIVES

ALWAYS BE ACTIVE, NOT PASSIVE

If there is anything that puts an audience off, it is a string of negatives. One is bad enough, especially when it comes at the beginning of a speech. It is amazing how many speakers put some kind of apology into their opening sentence. Never do it. No matter what you feel like apologizing for, always kick off with a positive. Anything less makes an audience aware of your lack of confidence.

Even when you require a negative in your speech for effect, take care that more do not keep slipping in. Your whole speech will leave a passive impression rather than a vigorous, active one if this occurs.

VISUAL NEGATIVES

Negatives infiltrate other sections of a presentation too. Sometimes it is the speaker's voice—hesitant, too low-key, nervous, or monotonous. A voice full of vitality seldom sinks into the realm of negativity.

The visual negative has its effect too. Some speakers turn up drably or unsuitably dressed. Poor grooming is another *No!*

INSECURITY

Negative body language is a real giveaway. Speakers who shuffle, scratch, keep clearing their throats, or stand in the defensive pose of crossed arms are displaying insecurity.

Perspiration on the forehead or under the arms is embarrassing. If there is any possibility of the former, make sure you have a handkerchief—not a tissue—in your pocket. Instead of dabbing continually, which is distracting, one good wipe will take the perspiration away for a much longer time. A strong antiperspirant should be used to prevent the latter.

THE ART

OF

INTRODUCING YOURSELF

OR

HAVING SOMEONE

DO IT FOR YOU

DON'T BE SHY!

Isn't it funny how self-conscious we can become when asked to give details about ourselves and our accomplishments? But if you want to survive in the tough world of public speaking you have to get over this.

The introduction is a vital part of your speech. Your audience has to know who you are, what you've done, why you've chosen that particular subject and what your credentials are for speaking about it.

BEING INTRODUCED

If someone else is ready to do the honors, give that person your introduction printed in large type or clearly handwritten and triple spaced. It has to be easy to read. If your name is difficult to pronounce, write it again in brackets, phonetically.

It always grates and frustrates when you hear your name mispronounced. If it is said incorrectly when you are introduced, correct it graciously and with humor. If you know who is going to introduce you in advance, send your introduction to them beforehand. This gives them time to practice and add to it if they wish. If you do, make sure you have a copy with you in case the first one gets mislaid.

ON YOUR OWN

If there's no one around to introduce you, you may have to do it yourself. Sorry though this state is, you've got to do it well. Forget about being embarrassed. State the facts calmly rather than arrogantly, with vitality. That paragraph or two can either get you off to a great start or trip you up and make what's to come seem (yawn, yawn!) so dreary.

Keep it reasonably brief. A boring introduction can turn an audience off your main topic. Prepare it with as much care as you would your speech. Practice and rehearse it.

THE KEY TO SUCCESS
YOUR STYLE OF PRESENTATION

THE MESSAGE AND THE MESSENGER

In your head you can have a marvelous message, full of information, humor or advice, but what counts is how you actually present it. Study how successful speakers approach and attack their subjects. Notice how they never begin with anything bland or too low key. They start with words that captivate, whether they are in the form of rhetorical questions or statements that arouse interest.

From then on, they introduce one idea after another so that their speech builds to a climax. They do it well because they know that every speech is a performance, a little—or a lot—of theater. You have to "play" to the audience, woo them, charm them.

INTANGIBLE LINK

From the moment you stand in front of an audience you must project a sense of affection, not fear—and it must be real, not phony. An audience needs to feel that you really want to be there. If you can establish this intangible link at the beginning by the warmth of your smile and introduction, it is going to do wonders for your presentation.

RECALL

It is a fact that most people have difficulty remembering what they hear. Your speech must be constructed and presented in such a way that the points you want to get across are heard, understood, and remembered by your audience. This can be done by the way you use your voice (read all about this in *The Power of Speech*), the word pictures you present, by repetition, and perhaps the addition of visuals. In any case, it must be done with style.

THE LECTERN

a

stand

for

holding

a

book

or

papers

TO HOLD OR NOT TO HOLD

A lectern is, to some, like an oasis in a desert of emptiness. It may only be two pieces of wood—one vertical, the other horizontal—but when you're faced with an empty stage or platform it is something strong, something firm, something to hold on to.

The dictionary tells us that the word *lectern* comes from late Latin *lectrum*, and ultimately from *legere*—to read, which gives it a sense of purpose and history. On a platform the lectern still has a vital role to play.

HANDLE AND HANDLER

No matter how ornate or plain a lectern may be, it's how you handle it that proclaims you to be an amateur or a professional speaker. And I use the word *handle* with serious intent.

The inexperienced grasp a lectern as if to save themselves from drowning, clutching it with white knuckles and sweaty palms. It's their savior, something to steady their shaking hands and hopefully their beating hearts. A professional stands behind a lectern and uses it as it was meant to be used—to hold notes or a complete speech. If it is touched it is done so lightly.

GIVEAWAY LEGS

It's not only the hands that proclaim nervousness, legs do so too. How many times have you seen a speaker at a lectern who performs strange contortions with his legs? Some, not satisfied with twisting their legs one way, disentangle them and twist them the other, often again and again. It has a hypnotic effect on an audience.

If a lectern is not high enough for you to read your speech from easily, ask that it be raised. If, however, it is so high that you can't be seen over it, demand that you be given something to stand on.

ARMS & THE MAN

(OR SHOULD IT BE WOMAN?)
I'LL START AGAIN...

ARMS & THE PERSON

FROM ENEMIES TO FRIENDS

Once I saw a person on stage introducing a group of speakers, hands behind head and arms sticking out like a butterfly's wings. I was so fascinated by the stance I didn't hear what was being said. Arms can be a distraction.

Obviously that was an unusual case, but the flailing of arms, the erratic movement of arms or the total non-use of them all take a listener's mind off your verbal message.

THE TWITCH

Arms have a strange way of revealing how we feel. They are often the only outward indication of nerves or tension. A person may appear confident and speak with confidence, but a twitch or two of the arms or the hands can paint a different picture.

Even before you go to the platform you are being observed. Clenched fists, rapid movements of the hands, ring twisting, arms constantly raising the hands to rub the nose, scratch an ear, or pat the hair can be giveaways of inner tension.

BE HAPPY

Don't look upon your arms as enemies. Control them. Use them to reinforce your message. Train yourself to discard the defensive pose of tightly folded arms (it stops you breathing properly, anyway). Study others. Discover how arms can display signs of fear, arrogance, nervousness, and smugness as well as enthusiasm, vitality, and confidence.

Make your arms your friends. They will certainly repay you.

THE COMFORT
OF THE
COMFORT ZONE

SHOULD YOU STAY

SAFELY

INSIDE IT

OR

BE BOLD

AND

TAKE IT WITH YOU?

BABY, IT'S COLD OUTSIDE!

The comfort zone is where you're at your best; you're among family and friends, people who love you and trust you. In it you do just about everything right, your confidence is high and you say what you think, do what you want. You use your voice well with plenty of vitality. Everyone is happy. But take one step beyond that comfort zone and the reality of the big world can hit you so hard that you want to run back to where you feel safe.

DREAD AND DISMAY

There are two ways you can handle this. The trap many people fall into is carrying on in the same way, but always feeling insecure unless they're in the company of people they know. Their lack of confidence in themselves is like a heavy weight that drags them down all the time. Speaking up even in a small group is bad enough, but having to speak in public is something that fills them with dread and dismay. Often they turn down wonderful opportunities because they just can't cope.

THE SECRET

If you want to be able to do everything you've always dreamed about—including becoming a public speaker—you don't leave your comfort zone at all. You take it with you!

You push and push and push the boundary of your comfort zone out until you feel secure and relaxed everywhere, doing everything, with everyone. It takes time and determination, courage and practice, but it can be done. Start small, study the professional tricks of the trade, and make yourself speak up. Train yourself to relax and never be discouraged. Most successful people have gone through the same traumas. They succeeded because they persevered—so can you.

TO SUCCEED AS A

PUBLIC SPEAKER

(OR ANYTHING ELSE IN LIFE)

YOU CAN ONLY RELY ON

ONE PERSON:

YOURSELF

YOU'RE ON YOUR OWN

Don't let those words scare you. Treat them as a challenge, because it is true that no matter who teaches you or how many books you read, success lies entirely within yourself when you start to speak.

That doesn't mean that you can't prepare. Obviously you prepare what you plan to say and how you'll say it. You must also prepare mentally for the occasion. The brain is like a computer. It accepts what you tell it without emotion. The better you program your brain, the greater chance you will have of living up to your expectations.

OUT WITH THE NEGATIVES

What you have to do first is discard all the negative messages you may have been programming in for years: "I sound dreadful," "I could never speak in public," "I'm too frightened to stand up before a crowd," and so on.

So, throw out, burn, or drown the mass of negatives you have been storing since childhood. Don't give them any chance of creeping in again to "comfort" you. In their place install the positives: "I sound great," "I can speak in public," and "I have the courage to stand up before a crowd."

DOESN'T COST A CENT

Keep it simple—the easier and simpler the better. Program the new thoughts into your brain all the time, every day, either by thinking them, speaking them out loud, or, better still, recording them. Reinforcement works wonders. It is one sure way of changing how you feel about yourself. It doesn't cost anything and you don't need anyone else to do it for you.

A FEW

MORE

P

P

P

P

P

Ps

P

P

P

P

P

P

TO PLAY WITH

66

THE POLISHED PERFORMANCE

In *The Power of Speech* I talk a lot about the six Ps—PITCH, PACE, PAUSE, POWER, PASSION, PROFESSIONALISM. These form the basis of all quality speech. Now I'd like to add a few more.

PREPARATION is an obvious one, yet some speakers simply do not do their homework, and it shows. Careful preparation of content and style can turn an ordinary topic into an extraordinary one.

PROTECTION is the name of this game. Protect yourself from offering half-baked ideas. Protect yourself from looking and sounding amateurish. Protect yourself from displaying fear and nerves.

POISE is what you must cultivate. The art of being in total control of yourself. Watch how the professionals do it. Many good speakers let themselves down by being clumsy in their movements.

You need to POLISH your speech. No aspect of it should be left to chance. There is nothing more frustrating than listening to a speaker mumble through an incoherent speech, full of vague references and muddled thinking—even a carefully planned speech needs polish.

Every speaker has to be able to judge the PULSE of an audience. Is it quickening? Slowing down? Dying? It is important to sense the pulse because then you have an opportunity to do something about it. You may even be able to inject a lifesaver when things are looking really sad.

The PERSONAL touch is always appreciated. I hear so many dreary speeches that ramble on about what other people think and do, without even a hint of the thoughts or emotions of the speaker. Don't overdo it, of course. Too heavy a personal load can be incredibly dreary.

THE FIRST
60
SECONDS

MAKE OR BREAK TIME

THE ONE-MINUTE KICKOFF

Never be fooled into thinking that you have the whole of the time allotted to you to conquer your audience. On the contrary, you're lucky if you survive the first 60 seconds.

Sounds tough, doesn't it?

It's a hard, inescapable fact about speaking in public: from the moment you stand up or walk onto a platform, your audience is summing you up. I want to impress upon you the importance of those vital seconds when you begin to speak.

THE "IF" SYNDROME

If your voice sounds weak or hesitant, if you stutter through your opening words, if you begin with old-fashioned phraseology, if you tell a dirty joke, if you are obviously ill prepared—if, if, if—your audience will immediately pick up unfortunate vibes and may begin to switch off.

No matter how good you are later, you will still have to battle hard to overcome the early damaging seconds. Those 60 seconds can be used to your advantage, to lift you up in your audience's opinion so that they want to hear more.

HOW DO YOU DO THAT?

Make sure you know exactly what your opening is to be. Make it warm, give it vitality, create an original theme for those first precious words.

Rehearse your introduction. Speak it out loud—over and over again. Become so familiar with the words that you could say them in your sleep, each time making sure that it sounds like you at your best and not like something you've learned by rote.

WHAT SHOULD YOU DO

IF

You can't breathe properly?

Your mouth is dry?

You start to shake?

CONTROLLING THE BODY

The physical signs of nervousness are common, but some simple practices can help relieve them. Most important is to prepare for your speech well beforehand, then you have a better chance of hiding them.

To be able to control your breathing on a platform, deep breathing exercises should be done daily. (For help, see *The Power of Speech*.) These are easy to do and greatly improve your breath control, as well as the quality of your voice. Before you go on stage, slip into the rest room and take a few deep breaths and hum. This will also help to steady your nerves.

DRYING UP

A dry mouth is another sign of nerves, and it can be frightening because you feel you won't be able to speak. Make sure you have a glass of water nearby on the platform, and take small sips if you need to. Don't gulp or that could cause you to sputter. Another tip is to gently bite the side of your tongue. This gives your saliva the message that it is needed for lubrication.

Some people suck a throat lozenge. That's fine, but make sure you have finished sucking, or get rid of it, before speaking. It is only too easy to swallow and get it stuck in your throat.

SHAKE, RATTLE, AND ROLL

We are always more conscious of the shakes than are the people who look at us. To us it seems as though our whole body is like jelly, but there are ways of calming ourselves down. If you have this problem, try these tips. Do some deep breathing. Put on a brave front. Walk tall. Smile—a smile is surprisingly relaxing. Speak authoritatively and don't gabble. Before long your shaking will stop and will be replaced by positive nervous energy.

T IS

BETTER

TO BE BRIEF

THAN TEDIOUS

William Shakespeare

BOX OF TRICKS

The old bard really knew what he was talking about, even though he didn't always practice it himself! There is so much wisdom in those few words they should be in every public speaker's box of tricks.

Let's take the last word first. The dictionary describes *tedious* as "tiresomely long; wearisome." The thesaurus adds words like *endless, monotonous, unvarying, prolonged, long-winded, fatiguing, exhausting, boring, dreary, dry as dust, drab, colorless, insipid, soporific, flat, banal, uninteresting, repetitious, mechanical,* and *soul-destroying.*

BE AWARE

Now you know why you don't want to be labeled as a tedious speaker! But to be sure you aren't, you must be aware of how you speak. Most of the tedious are not aware of how they sound and that's why they drone on the way they do. Learn to listen. Learn to listen intelligently. Don't ridicule yourself and lose faith, just use the listening process as a way to improve—every time you speak.

KEEP TO THE POINT

Brief. That word must be used intelligently too. In this context it does not mean abrupt or brusque, get it over with quick, or I'm not interested. It does mean concise, succinct, keep to the point, don't ramble, and hold your audience.

It is a pleasure to listen to speakers who do keep to the point, who use brevity to enhance their speeches, who put as much vitality and interest into minutes as the tedious might give to an hour or more.

Guess who the winners are.

THE ART OF

KEEPING THE

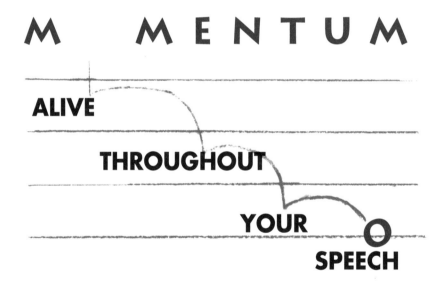

M   MENTUM

ALIVE

THROUGHOUT

YOUR

SPEECH

AFTER THE FLYING START

You're off! Your speech is sounding great. The audience looks interested. They're listening and watching attentively. The adrenalin is pumping through you. Nothing can harm you now.

Or can it? A good beginning is essential, but the impetus, the energy, the propulsion, the drive, the thrust, and the spark must be there all the way through.

SENSITIVITY

Even as you speak you must be aware of a change in your listeners' interest. If it diminishes and you sense a restlessness, then you are doing something wrong. The most likely causes are (1) your voice is dropping into a monotone; (2) the gabble is taking hold; (3) your ability to instill that touch of magic into your speech is fading; or (4) you've become so focused on the words you're saying, you have forgotten that words may sound meaningless unless they are expressed with vitality.

UNDOING THE DAMAGE

When you suddenly realize that you have lost your audience, what should you do? Try this: STOP. Look at your audience. Make them look at you. Try taking in one or two deep breaths to fill your lungs with oxygen. This makes you feel more alive.

Your task now is to undo the damage you've already done. You can't plead, "Please listen to me!" You have to regain their interest by starting again with a much more interesting voice.

That voice must have strength and the vitality that's been missing. Slow down. Use your pauses. Accentuate the important words in your speech, and make them capture its mood. The turnaround must occur if you're to succeed.

ARE YOUR SPEECHES

INFORMATIVE?

Funny?

EGO Trips?

TIME WASTERS?

BORING?

STIMULATING?

Passionate ?

MEMORABLE?

COURAGE AND DEDICATION

No doubt you'd like your speeches to be described by at least some of these words, especially *memorable*, *informative*, and perhaps *passionate*, but certainly not *boring* or *time wasters*.

The trouble is that the very people who are boring usually are the ones who aren't aware of it, and they continue to bore the socks off their audiences for years. So this is one of the first aspects of public speaking you have to tackle. Ask yourself, "How do my audiences react to my speeches?"

A BRAVE HEART

It takes courage to acknowledge that you may indeed be less than acceptable. It takes dedication to study other people when you have so many problems of your own to contend with. But it is these attributes that help you to succeed in the end.

Forget about yourself. You've done your homework, you've rehearsed, you've got yourself in front of an audience. Now is the time to take note of how that audience is accepting you.

Don't get paranoid about it. Just be aware of your audience as individuals as well as a whole.

WOO THEM

Play to the audience, woo them. Let them know your first objective is to give them what they want. Audiences tend to get irritated if they feel speakers are there only to talk at them or to bolster their own self-image. Rapport between an audience and a speaker is one of the joys of public speaking.

WHAT SHOULD YOU DO

IF

You forget your words?

You hear yourself gabbling?

You lose your place?

O O O

TIPS TO TREASURE

I always treasure the mass of little tips on public speaking I've picked up over the years. They can make the difference between doing well and doing brilliantly. In their own way they can reinforce your confidence or take it away.

Forgetting your words when you're on a platform can be devastating—it can really throw you. Your brain goes numb. It makes all the things you planned to say disappear, so you've got to break the pattern. I find that admitting the problem helps you relax. Your audience understands. Every single person has done it at some time or another. I say, "I was just about to tell you something but I can't think what it is! Never mind. It'll come back." And it always does.

THE GABBLE

So often when we're nervous, we belt out our words at breakneck speed. Even on a stage listen to yourself. As soon as you know you're going too fast—STOP! Then SLOW DOWN. Your audience would far rather have you do that than strain to listen to a garbled speech they may not fully understand. The slowing down also helps you to move into your prepared pattern of speech. This bolsters your confidence.

LOSING YOUR PLACE

If you've written out your speech, it is always possible that you could lose your place when you're speaking, so protect yourself against this happening. It is all in the way you prepare your pages. Handwriting or a typeface that is too small, or lines too close together, make it very difficult to look up and then find your place again. (See pages 36–37 for ideas.)

THE CONCLUSION

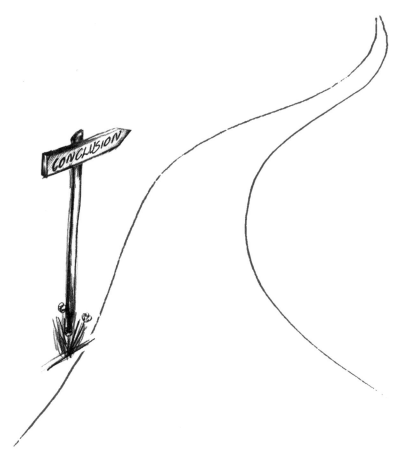

IS AS IMPORTANT AS THE OPENING

THE CLIMAX COUNTS

The final minutes of a speech are no time to think, "Thank goodness, it's all over!" If you do, the chances are that you'll rush, forget how important it is to hold your audience, and let your speech drift off into nothingness.

Those last words are precious. They make a deep impression on an audience. They can express in a punchy way your personality, your way with words, your thoughts, and your arguments.

SHORT AND SHARP

Your conclusion shouldn't be long-winded. It has to be concise yet bring your speech to a climax. This is not the time for new thoughts or ideas, rather it is the time for summing up what you have already said.

You started with a strong and meaningful opening. In your conclusion you can refer back to that and quickly show how you developed your theme by outlining the main points of your speech and reminding your audience of some specific points.

OPTIMISM

Slow down for your conclusion. Use words and phrases with rhythm and imagination. Be a little dramatic if you wish. This is the time when you want to leave your audience knowing that you really are a performer. Throw them a compliment, offer encouragement, perhaps real optimism. Invite them to consider or take action. Never end on a negative, either in voice or content.

Don't let the thought of ending make you careless. It is how you speak from start to finish that ensures you will be invited back.

YOUR SPEECH IS OVER

NOW

IT'S

QUESTION
& ANSWER TIME

ON THE FINAL LAP

The relief at having got through your speech can leave you vulnerable for the follow-up session. Don't relax yet. Remember you are still being judged. Keep your mind sharp and stay calm.

Listen carefully when a question is asked. Let the audience sense that you take it seriously. Establish eye contact with the questioner, then look around the audience as you reply. Answer to the best of your ability, but keep it simple and direct. Don't go on too long.

REPEAT THE QUESTION

Often people ask a question in a voice that cannot be heard by others in the room, so repeat the question. This also gives you time to think of a reply. If you don't know the answer, say so. It is better to be honest than to make up an answer that fools no one.

Your attitude to questioners is important. Some speakers treat them with contempt, which does not go down well with audiences. Every question is important to the person asking it. Even if you regard a question as foolish, reply with courtesy if nothing else.

THE SPARK

If no one is brave enough to ask a question and you have allotted time to the session, start by asking yourself one. When you have answered that, you can then look at your audience and ask them a question. Usually someone will reply and that can spark others to ask the questions they were hoping to ask anyway.

If they don't, just add a few more thoughts of your own and bring the meeting to a close by summarizing your speech.

QUESTION & ANSWER

PROBLEM TIME

NO BULLYING HERE PLEASE

Question time can be as harrowing as the speech itself. If you are in an aggressive or even hostile environment you may have left yourself open to criticism by what you have said. It is most important that you remain calm and answer carefully. Don't let any questioner rattle you, no matter how abusive he or she may be. If you don't agree, say so firmly. You can always add, "Of course, you're entitled to your opinion."

If someone makes a good point—one you may not have thought of before—say so. This takes away aggression quicker than a wink!

THREE INSTEAD OF ONE

Questioners have a tendency to ask two or even three questions at once. Clarify this by asking which question they would like answered. Sometimes questioners are almost incoherent. If you don't understand what they're trying to say, ask them politely to be more specific.

If questioners interrupt your answers, don't talk over them. Let them finish, then complete your answer. Never allow a questioner to give a "speech." Simply cut in and ask for their question.

NOT TRUE

If a questioner twists your words and comes out with a statement that is not true, correct the information, then deal with the question as you see it.

Don't let anyone in the audience bully you. Be firm but be tactful. If they persist with a question, suggest you talk it over later.

Beware of making rash promises. It is an easy way out at the time, but you may regret it later.

TRAIN YOURSELF TO SPEAK WITHOUT NOTES

I want you to do something for me

Here is a word

Moon

(as in the sky)

Think about it

Write down as many
words you associate
with the moon
as you can

Take about a minute

BEGIN NOW!

LESSON IN LOGIC

If you're like most people, you've included in your list words like *yellow, stars, blue cheese, crescent, man-in-the-moon, tides, sky, moonlight, rocket, moon river, craters, astronaut, eclipse, lady of the night, rotation, moonbeam, bright, weightlessness,* and so on. That's fine. Except a list like this is all *jumbled up*. It jumps from one image to another. There's no *pattern* to it.

If you were trying to convey information about the moon to someone what chance would they have of making any sense of it? Very little, I expect.

THE CHART

Now I'd like you to look at the next page and see how I've recorded my words about the moon. I've drawn a chart with a circle in the middle. On the outside of the circle, the chart is rather like a clock, so it's important that we have a line at 12 o'clock, a quarter past, half past, and a quarter to, plus as many other divisions as we may need.

You'll see that I've put the word *moon* in the *middle*. Then in the space following the 12 o'clock line (we always start there) I've entered the words I feel are the first I need to describe the moon itself. Then, in a logical manner, I've gone clockwise and built up my picture, section by section, so that a listener could follow my reasoning. In every case—and this is important—I've put a title or heading at the top of the divisions and <u>underlined</u> it. I call these sections *categories*.

A CLEAR WORD PICTURE

Look at the chart again. If I placed the words haphazardly from different categories, I'd end up with a list as jumbled as before. By giving each category its rightful place in my chart I can present a clear picture by simply glancing at the chart. Try making your own chart and entering your list of words—under their category headings—and see how much clearer your word picture is.

THE MOON

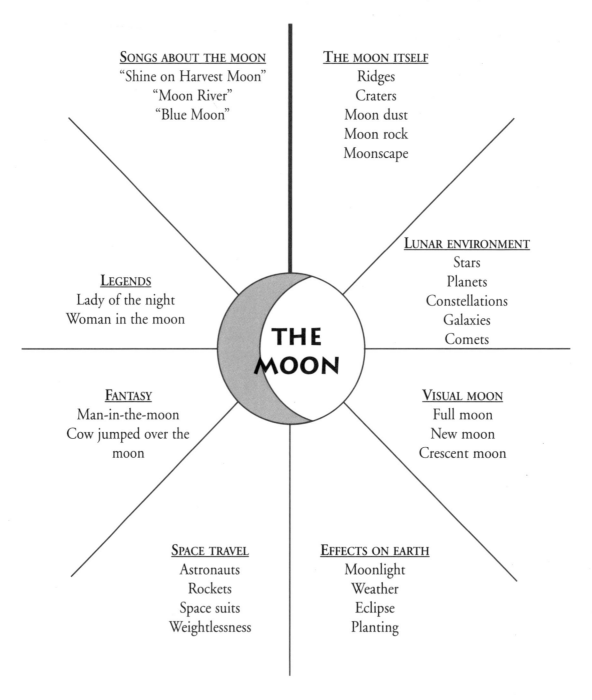

SONGS ABOUT THE MOON
"Shine on Harvest Moon"
"Moon River"
"Blue Moon"

THE MOON ITSELF
Ridges
Craters
Moon dust
Moon rock
Moonscape

LEGENDS
Lady of the night
Woman in the moon

LUNAR ENVIRONMENT
Stars
Planets
Constellations
Galaxies
Comets

THE MOON

FANTASY
Man-in-the-moon
Cow jumped over the
moon

VISUAL MOON
Full moon
New moon
Crescent moon

SPACE TRAVEL
Astronauts
Rockets
Space suits
Weightlessness

EFFECTS ON EARTH
Moonlight
Weather
Eclipse
Planting

SIMPLICITY ITSELF

What you now do is use the same "moon chart" when you have to give a *speech*. Where I put the word *moon* in the first chart, you now record the title of your talk. By thinking out the overall plan of your speech, you break it up into categories, underline the headings, and add as many key words as you wish in each section. The beauty of this is that when you give your speech, you only have one piece of paper. A glance now and then is all you need.

I've frequently seen people sit in front of my video camera and try to talk on a subject they know well. They fail because they get muddled in their thinking and there's no logic to what they say. Their talk peters out after a minute or two.

THEY'RE OFF!

Then I show them the moon chart and instruct them how to use it. Having studied it, they can immediately speak on the same subject confidently and rationally for ten minutes or more. It's exciting to watch.

Another plus is the fact that you can prepare material on a variety of subjects— for meetings, conferences, or whatever—and file them away to be used at any time. It saves a lot of work not having to think out the subject again and again. People use it for essays, documents, working out plots for stories and books. I like it because it's so easy to use. If you know your subject, you only need the key words.

NO NOTES

Because I don't use notes or a script when I speak, it may seem as though everything is totally spontaneous. But the best speeches are not. They're carefully planned.

So I do my planning on a moon chart before I go. Sometimes I use several; crossing out, changing categories and key words around, working out which is the most logical order to use. When I'm happy, I photograph the final moon chart in my mind, and then leave it behind.

YOUR MOON CHART

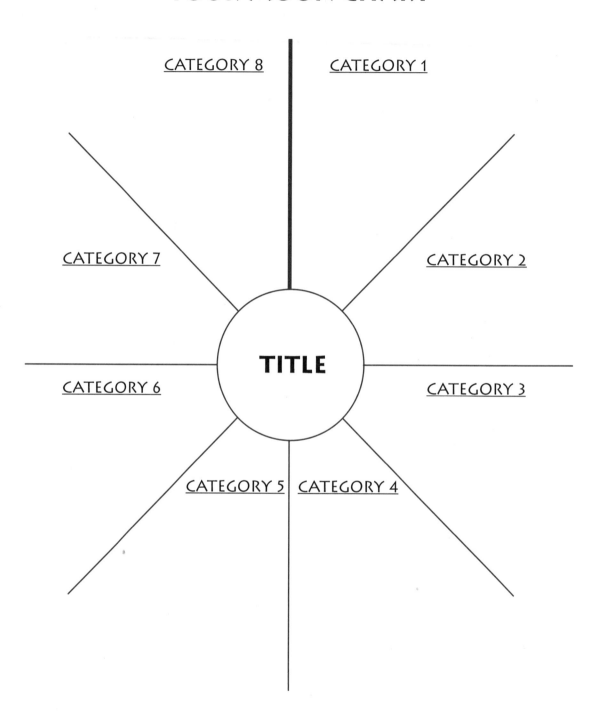

CATEGORY 8

CATEGORY 1

CATEGORY 7

CATEGORY 2

TITLE

CATEGORY 6

CATEGORY 3

CATEGORY 5

CATEGORY 4

WHAT TO DO WITH IT

Now that you've got your own moon chart, start using it. Practice with a variety of subjects.

The word I always start people off with is *road*. Sounds easy, doesn't it? Yet by the time they have finished with it, most of them are amazed at the long list of both categories and key words they have compiled, from what a road is made from, to people who use it, to the abstract.

ROAD

<u>Construction</u>—concrete, asphalt, gravel, paved, dirt, cobblestone...

<u>Names</u>—street, avenue, boulevard, drive, lane, terrace, circle, court...

<u>Markings</u>—parking lines, yellow lines, double lines, crossings, arrows...

<u>Signs</u>—stop, caution, children crossing, railroad crossing, school...

<u>Vehicles</u>—cars, vans, trailers, trucks, buses, caravans, motorcycles...

<u>People</u> – business people, tourists, joggers, hikers, police, bikers...

<u>Functions</u>—transport, communication, physical fitness, freight...

<u>Animals</u>—dogs, cats, horses, cattle, sheep, raccoons, rabbits, frogs...

<u>Scenery</u>—gardens, houses, churches, shops, fields, farms, rivers...

<u>Plants</u>—trees, hedges, grass, weeds, flowers, wild flowers, shrubs...

<u>Roadwork</u>—shovels, bulldozers, concrete mixers, water trucks, flags...

<u>Accessories</u>—footpaths, drains, underground cables, curbs, poles...

<u>Rules</u>—traffic law, speed limits, age limits, blood alcohol limit, vehicles...

<u>Accidents</u>—crashes, collisions, speed, alcohol, pedestrians, fatigue...

<u>Road breaks</u>—railroads, bridges, intersections, cattle crossings, barriers...

<u>Songs</u>—"Road to Morocco," "Rocky Road," "Yellowbrick Road"....

<u>Abstract</u>—Road to Knowledge, Road to Freedom, Road to Success...

TELEVISION

HAS

A LOT

TO

ANSWER

FOR,

BUT

DON'T

LET IT

BEAT

YOU

THE OTHER SIDE OF TV

Whether you like it or not, television has a big role to play in the way you come across to your audience. Why? Because everyone in that audience will have been brainwashed by television whether they like it or not. Even those who say that they hate television have become accustomed to having a television set in their homes. They've got used to the immediate flow of news, documentaries, game shows, dramas, soap operas, advertisements—and to the shortened attention span needed for them.

DANGER!

Audiences will not put up with long, boring speeches. They have been programmed to respond to short, sharp bursts of information, quick changes of scenery, to the sound of professionals, to sound bites.

Your audience may not know why, but their inner ears will tell them that you are not worth listening to unless you give them what they want—colorful, vibrant speech, flowing language, entertaining ideas, and a speech that holds their attention every second you are on the platform.

TO HAM IT UP OR NOT TO HAM IT UP

Don't feel that you have to go overboard and ham everything up in order to be interesting. On the contrary, the "ham" is just as irritating as the "bore."

What you do need is an interesting subject, a style of delivery that captures attention from the moment you open your mouth, and the confidence to carry it through to the end. Within that structure you must be aware of recapturing their attention every few minutes. Pepper your speech with little "hooks." It's always better to leave them wanting more than to watch them wilt before your eyes.

SOME
PITFALLS
OF

PRESENTATION

Talking down

Not listening

R^ambling

SELF-APPRAISAL

One of the most elementary truths aspiring speakers have to learn is how to respect the intelligence and integrity of their audiences. They also have to discover how, in turn, they can win their audiences' respect. Many times I have sat in an auditorium and become enraged by a speaker's arrogance and indifference to the audience.

Talking down is, I believe, one of the great sins of public speaking. The worst offenders, unfortunately, are usually so opinionated they don't realize how irritating they are.

BEING AWARE

Looking at yourself critically is not easy, yet it has to be done. Become aware of your audience's reaction every time you speak, analyze your performance and be aware of how you present your material—conscious even of the tone of voice you use.

Listen as well as speak. Absorb the murmurs of approval, the rattles of discontent, the shuffles of boredom. Next time make the percentages go in your favor. Raise your antenna and sense the feeling of the room before it is too late. Like so much in life, practice makes perfect.

THE BIG YAWN

A short, snappy speech is always more acceptable than a long, boring one. You may feel you have to keep going on and on to get your information across, but you can always edit or shorten the speech and nobody will know the difference. We all tend to put far too much into a single speech, expect our audience to remember each point, and end up frustrating them.

SOME MORE PITFALLS

gobbledygook

jargon

gibberish

hogwash

TOO SLICK FOR COMFORT

You have only to listen to some politicians, civic dignitaries and the like to know that the era of double-talk is not dead. Study, if you can, the confused way they construct their speeches, their use of obscure phraseology and the way they leave you unsure of what they were getting at in the first place.

I love the whimsical word *gobbledygook*. It is almost onomatopoeic, suggesting a mouth full of *gobble*. Unfortunately, too many people have an element of it when they make a speech.

SIMPLICITY

An unspoken rule for all speakers is to be understood. When you're planning and preparing your speech, from the very beginning make sure that each idea, each phrase, each statement is simple. Remember that your audience will only hear it once. They can't put up their hands and ask you to repeat yourself.

Weed out any sign of pretentiousness. Watch out for pomposity. Weigh what you want to say against the way that you'll say it, and throw jargon to the wind. Technical language should only be used within a confined audience of totally like-minded people. To anyone else it is gibberish.

ON TARGET

To avoid including even a touch of hogwash, make the time and effort to plan your speech carefully. Write down the main points you want to get across. Make sure they follow each other logically so that people can follow your meaning. Fill in the detail, but only as much as you know they can take in at one time.

HOW DOES A

SPECH

COMPARE

TO

EVERYDAY

TALKING?

FROM COTTON TO SILK

Everyday speech is filled with language that flows out of us effortlessly, with chatter, sometimes a little gossip. It's easy, fun, and we don't have to worry about what we'll say next. If we make a mistake, who cares? The whole arena of everyday talk is uncomplicated—no matter what mood we might be in.

STANDING UP

The moment we stand up and speak out in front of people, so much of what we take for granted deserts us. Words stick in the throat, breathing becomes erratic, memory can fail, and confidence takes a nose dive.

It is important to realize that every action involved in public speaking can be improved. You may never become an orator, but you certainly could progress to the level of extreme competency.

The answer lies within yourself.

TIRELESS EFFORT

Are you prepared to put some effort into this most necessary of skills? Are you prepared to put yourself into a learning situation no matter what your age or education? Are you prepared to risk being made to feel a little bit silly at first to advance toward the goal of being a good public speaker?

Many an outstanding speaker will tell you of the effort they put into their early speeches, of their disappointments as well as their successes. They didn't start out being brilliant. They had to learn, to progress in order to discover the secrets.

It is so important not to become discouraged. The hardest part is taking the first step.

THE TRAP

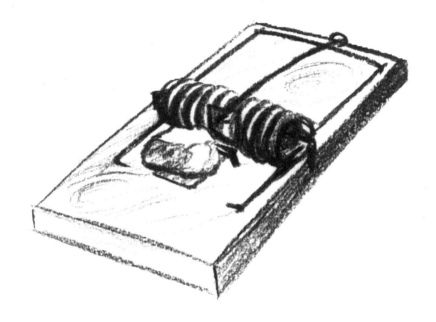

TRYING TO

SPEAK

THE WRITTEN WORDS

SPEAK UP AND SPEAK OUT

Speaking written words is fine, provided your written words have been prepared for speech. If they have been put into written language designed for the eye, then you cannot deliver them with the ease and flowing style required for the voice. As I emphasized in *The Power of Speech*, what looks good to the eye can offend the ear.

KEEP IT SIMPLE

In speech we use contractions. We say, "I'm sure you're right," "He's very successful," "It's been a long time," "I won't be long," "She mustn't do that," "We aren't coming today."

Words like *anticipate*, *participate*, and *endeavor* are written style ones. Could you imagine going home and saying to your family, "I'll endeavor to paint that room tomorrow"? Of course not; they'd think you were crazy. You're more likely to say, "I'll try..."

On the written page we often write long, complicated sentences, but if we try to speak them, we can run into all sorts of problems. We sound stilted and old fashioned and what we say does not have a natural ring. We also have to be careful of tongue twisters—words that trip us up.

THE VERNACULAR

When you listen to good speech, you'll hear words and phrases that flow effortlessly. Sometimes they are ungrammatical, colloquial, and include the vernacular. But this is how we speak.

Study your script for any hint of formality. Speak it aloud over and over again. This is the only way you'll get the feel of the spoken word. Become your own editor, but be a tough one.

THE PLACE
OF HUMOR

IN PUBLIC
SPEAKING

LAUGHTER OR LASSITUDE

Nothing turns us off more quickly than an unfunny, trying-to-be-funny speaker. But if the trying-to-be-funny speaker has a natural flow of humor that's great. We all love a laugh, and a touch of humor has certainly brightened up many an otherwise tedious performance.

FLASH POINT

There are different levels of humor. As a speaker, you have to be aware of what your particular level is. With a little deviousness a speaker may cover up lack of preparation or a slim amount of knowledge, but with humor, what they hear is what you've got. Fun that falls flat deflates a speaker in a flash.

To reach the hilarious stage you need to be a born comedian. True comedians have only to look at an audience to have them burst into helpless laughter. Next to them are those who can tell a story superbly. Every nuance, every twist and turn of it is there to savor and delight. They can make even mundane subjects come to life.

SEXIST IS OUT!

Don't be disheartened. The average speaker can tell a very acceptable joke or story that puts a spark into his speech. It is the below average humorist who bugs most of us. If a speaker begins with a tasteless or badly told joke, his chance of acceptance overall gets off to a poor start. Sexist, ethnic, and sleazy jokes are out. So is a joke where the end lacks a punch.

Try out your stories or jokes on your friends. See how they relate. Do they laugh or seem embarrassed? Practice until you can confidently tell about a funny incident or a particular joke easily and with vitality. Next time you speak in public, try out your skill. If it works, you'll know you're on the way to becoming the entertaining speaker we all long to be.

SPEECHES
REFLECT THE FOUR SEASONS

WELL, THREE OUT OF FOUR

It's spring! Everyone is longing to hear you. There is an eagerness, a feeling of anticipation, a new beginning. Just as the earth provides flowers with the means to grow and blossom, you are all set to deliver an exciting, interesting, and informative talk that will enrich your audience and make them feel it was worth coming to hear you.

The first minutes should captivate them, lead them towards the main thrust of your speech with a vitality that they will respond to—just as we all respond to the first growth of a new year.

SUPER SUMMER

As they warm to you, the temperature of your speech should rise, like the thermometer in summer. This is the period of the year when we're relaxed, happy, outgoing, full of energy and activity. It is the fun time, the time for entertaining. Your speech should reflect this. There should be a bond between you and your audience that makes them almost bask in your words and the way you deliver them.

HARVEST

Just as autumn comes, you should now be ready to reap your harvest. You've planted ideas, nurtured them, given your best, supplied your audience with information, and entertained them. Your speech has matured.

Ideally, speeches should end with autumn. Unfortunately, often they do not. If their pace falters, many speakers drift prematurely into a cold and wintery world where the audience feels trapped and wish they had not come. At the very hint of winter, double back to the idyllic days of summer!

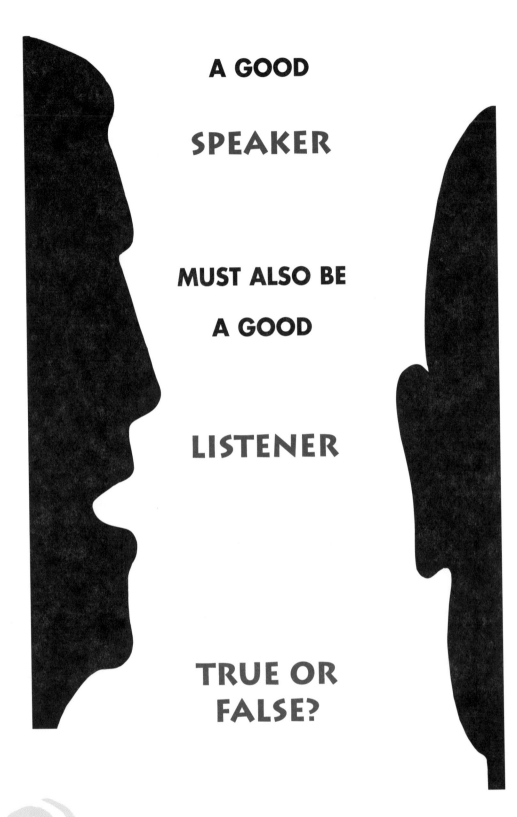

A GOOD

SPEAKER

MUST ALSO BE
A GOOD

LISTENER

TRUE OR
FALSE?

ONLY TOO TRUE

One reason why some people never make the big time as speakers is that they do not listen. I'm not talking about delivery here—the listening and analyzing of speech—but listening to what other people actually say.

If you have aspirations as a leader—even if it is just within a small organization, it is imperative that you use your powers of deduction and judgment when others speak.

BOTH SIDES

In a debate, each speaker must listen carefully to the theories, facts, and opinions that the opposing team puts forward. It is important to be able to quickly and ably refute an argument or produce a better one. The audience can then consider both sides before making up its mind.

As a speaker, you do not have to be in a debate to do this. If you are alert, you can pick up what other speakers are saying during a conference, comments from the chair or even from the person who introduces you. To be able to add more material, change tack, be flexible, and introduce new thoughts, takes not only courage but considerable expertise.

ADRENALIN

Inexperienced speakers, with prepared material, often cannot do this. Their nervousness hampers their performance. It is frustrating to listen to a speaker who ignores relevant information and keeps doggedly on with her own material. This is one more reason why you must aim to be as flexible as possible.

Listening also helps to raise your adrenaline and your performance. You're waiting for your turn to speak and you think to yourself, "I could do better that that!"

THAT

INVISIBLE

PERSONALITY

COULD IT BE YOU?

SOMEBODY ELSE

If there is one thing I don't like, it is listening to speakers who sound unnatural. I don't mean what happens when people have an attack of nerves, but when they actually *change* their personality on a platform, on television, or when among important people.

Public figures sometimes get coached to improve their presentations. This is fine—provided it doesn't change the type of people they are. We often hear them pontificating on a platform, making all the right sounds and doing the correct gestures, but they come across as phonies.

HEARTFELT

Why? Because quality speech comes from the heart. This doesn't mean we can't improve. Of course we can. It is vital to absorb every trick possible, but by *trick* I don't mean something artificial. Speech is filled with tricks of the trade, ways of taking what is already there and making it better and Better and BETTER.

Always beware of trying too hard. The overeager often turn out performances that sound stilted, stiff, forced, and pretentious. Even learned body language can be affected. Movements become wooden and clumsy. People might ask, "Where is the real person?"

UNIQUE

Seek advice, take advice, but make sure you absorb it into your own personality. I realize the difficulty when you are faced with indecision and nervousness. It is only too easy to cover up by putting on a front. But that front may not be you. There is only one you. You are unique. Make sure you stay that way.

THE REQUISITES OF

LEADERSHIP
"WITH WORDS WE GOVERN MEN"

Benjamin Disraeli

A TALL ORDER

The requisites of leadership are many and varied. They include intelligence, determination, competence, ambition, imagination, vision, commitment, honesty, dependability, motivation, inspiration, courage, and loyalty—to name but a few.

To be a great leader that list must also include the ability to communicate. We communicate in many ways—one to one, one to a few, one to many, and so on. Unfortunately, many ambitious high flyers don't realize how powerful good speech can be.

WHY?

Why is it that so many of our leaders in so many walks of life have not yet appreciated this most obvious of goals?

Why is it that these uncommonly intelligent and, in their own fields, extremely professional people produce such boring speeches?

Why is it that people like me, who are called in to train them, find that their knowledge of the skills of public speaking is elementary?

Why is it that when a breakthrough comes, the reaction is "Why have I wasted all this time? I should have learned this at school."

FROM UNDERPRIVILEGED TO PRIME MINISTER

Disraeli's thoughts are apt. He knew only too well the truth behind his statement. He belonged to the wrong class, race, religion, and educational background, yet because he added the power of words to his genius he became Prime Minister of Britain in the 19th century. Perhaps being a novelist in his early days gave him a feeling for language.

If you have aspirations of leadership, don't waste time.

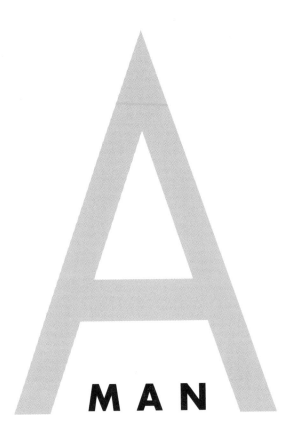

A

MAN

should never be ashamed to own
he has been in the wrong, which is
saying in other words, that he is
wiser today than he was
yesterday.

ALEXANDER POPE

FROM RIGHT TO WRONG—
AND BACK AGAIN

The content of your speech belongs entirely to you. You can be shown how to prepare it, deliver it, and later analyze it, but what you decide to say comes from your own experience, attitude, and values.

We all make mistakes in what we say occasionally. At the time we may not realize it. We make mistakes either by not checking facts or by having an opinion that we later change.

COMPLETE BLOCKHEADS

When we discover that we are in the wrong, the obvious thing is to admit it, yet that act is extremely difficult, if not impossible, for many people.

Having to admit that they were wrong, made a mistake, didn't fully understand the situation, messed things up, or were downright foolish, can make some people feel inadequate, open to ridicule, or appear as complete blockheads.

NO COVER-UP

Alexander Pope hit it right on the head. He who has the confidence and the integrity to admit being in the wrong will to most people appear "wiser today than he was yesterday."

So never be afraid to admit a mistake. If more people in high offices, as well as those in humbler positions, did so, we would have more faith in them and what they represent. Nothing irritates the public more than to hear about an attempted cover-up.

You can win an amazing amount of sympathy by being truthful—just remember how you respect others who are.

YOU CAN LEARN A LOT ABOUT

PUBLIC SPEAKING

BY SITTING IN THE AUDIENCE

LOOKING

LISTENING

LEARNING

ANALYZING

STUDYING

D.I.S.S.E.C.T.I.N.G

THE EYES HAVE IT

Sitting comfortably in the audience with no fear of having to make a good impression is an easy way to evaluate public speakers. After all, you are the reason why the speakers are there at all. Your appreciation—or lack of it—can make or break them. Your power is immense.

It is interesting to speak to members of an audience after a speech has been delivered. Everyone has an opinion and each opinion differs. People notice such a wide variety of things—how the speaker stood, the way he or she hopped from foot to foot, how he rubbed his nose and didn't look at the audience enough, the shuffling of her notes, what she was wearing, how her colors clashed… I could go on and on.

THE NITTY GRITTY

Although important, none of these are as far reaching as your opinion of the way the speaker spoke.

Criticism generally focuses on the pace. The average speaker dashes off information too quickly, not giving the audience time to digest it. This is especially true if that information contains facts and figures, which become meaningless if they are not grasped correctly. How often have you seen listeners try to take notes and then give up in frustration?

THE JUMPER

A speaker whose ideas don't flow well or seem disjointed is another source of irritation. You feel cheated, can't concentrate, and wonder why you've come. At first you are puzzled, then exasperated, when the speaker jumps from one subject to another then back again. Study speakers, but take to heart what you learn and don't make the same mistakes yourself.

YOU'VE JUST LISTENED TO SOME MARVELOUS

S P E E C H E S

THEY CAPTURED YOUR IMAGINATION AND
HELD YOUR ATTENTION FROM BEGINNING TO END

THEY SEEMED SO EFFORTLESS

HOW DID THEY DO IT?

THE CONSUMMATE PROFESSIONALS

To hear people of such caliber is a privilege. There aren't many of them around. As role models they are certainly worth studying. Analyze them, their style, and their speech. Try to capture that elusive quality that sets them apart from the average competent speaker. It isn't easy. Their vocal brilliance can often be difficult to define because it does indeed sound so effortless.

THE MARK

Yet that is the mark of professionals in any occupation or sphere. They make everything they say or do surprisingly simple and we are taken in by it. But try it ourselves and we immediately fall into all kinds of traps. Don't try to copy your role models, but study their techniques, their delivery, and their construction of speeches.

PROBE

First be aware of their voices—the pitch, the pace, the use of pauses. Take note of the power and the passion they put into their subjects.

Listen intently to the way they use language. Language can be dull or sparkling, humdrum or imaginative. The way people use words gives you a good indication as to their background, their thinking, their philosophy.

Study how they present their speeches. Are the openings strong—the type that hooks you and makes you want more? Is there plenty of information and challenge in the middle? When the speeches come to an end are you left satisfied yet wanting more?

Don't forget to look at their body language and see how their spoken and silent languages blend to create the images that make their speeches so memorable.

YOU'VE MADE A MAGNIFICENT SPEECH NOW YOU'RE ON THE RECEIVING END OF

PRAISE

ACCLAIM

&

COMPLIMENTS

HOW DO YOU RESPOND?

ACCEPTING PRAISE

When you succeed, you have to be able to accept praise in a calm and professional way. Many people cannot do this. How often have you gone up to compliment someone only to have them rave on about how terrible they were?

They are so overwhelmed at being noticed they undo all the good that they have achieved. Praise has a strange effect on some people; it shows up their insecurities, lack of confidence, and feelings of self-doubt.

TOPSY-TURVY

Praise brings out extraordinary body language too. People being praised may hang their heads and giggle, shrug their shoulders, or shake their heads. It is as though the thought of being successful is more than they can bear.

Watch these people and see how amateurish their reaction to a compliment is. Then make a pact with yourself never to behave in the same manner.

SO SIMPLE

When you know you deserve praise and someone gives it to you, all you have to do is say, "Thank you." It is as easy as that. If they persist, don't be afraid to discuss what you've said with them; they are obviously interested.

Your body language should be calm: smile, discuss the subject objectively, enjoy the moment, be appreciative, answer any questions.

The big no-no is to over react. No one likes the person with a swollen head, the "I'm-so-clever" attitude, or a contemptuous manner.

Never be afraid to sincerely praise people if you have really enjoyed their speeches—praise is always valued.

THE

THING

THAT

SPEAKERS

LOVE

TO

HATE

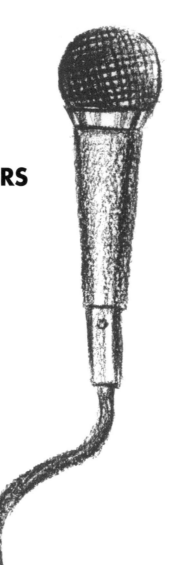

VOLUME OR VICTIM

No matter how great your speech is, if you can't be heard it is all for nothing, so a microphone is essential. Many speeches are ruined by speakers not knowing how to use microphones. Never blow into microphones, as you deposit moisture in them. Don't tap them or fiddle with them as you could cause those ear-splitting noises. When you stand too far away, the microphone will not pick up your voice. Stand too close and it could emphasize your explosive, sibilant sounds so that you seem to be hissing. Keep about 12 inches (30 cm) away, but adjust the distance if necessary.

ASK

If there is a technician present ask for instruction, but you may have to cope with it yourself. Watch how experienced speakers handle microphones.

First they find out whether the microphone they have to use is directional—one way only—or multidirectional. This information lets them know if they can move away from the microphone and still be heard.

They usually don't ask, "Can you hear me?" which is amateurish, but quickly sense if the audience is not hearing what they say by watching them. People screw up their faces and strain to catch sound when the reception is poor.

WALKING AROUND

Often speakers like to take microphones out from their stands and walk around with them. This is fine, provided they can get them out easily. Before you speak, see how the microphone is connected. This will save time when you need to detach it. A lapel microphone may be the answer if one is available. It certainly allows greater movement.

ENHANCE OR

RUIN A SPEECH

with the

FLICK

of a

SWITCH

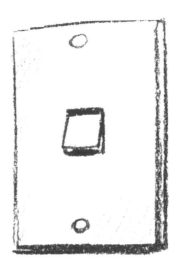

VISUALS—AID OR ANGUISH?

Some speakers won't speak without the backup of visual aids; some speakers freak out at the thought of using them. The sensible solution lies in between. If a speech really doesn't need visuals, why bother? If a speech could be improved with a visual aid that adds information, emphasis, color, or variety, why not?

THE EYES AND THE EARS

The main thing to remember is that a speech is absorbed through the ears. A visual is obviously for the eyes. The two must not come into conflict. Many otherwise excellent speeches have been ruined by the intrusion of visuals, speakers turning their backs on their audiences or standing in front of the very items that are supposed to help them.

Visuals need to be large enough for everyone to see, with simple wording or images, and should be well lit. Whether they're whiteboards, flip charts, transparencies, slides, storyboards, or display panels, speakers must know how to use them so that they are aids and not distractions.

AUDIOVISUALS

Here we have the combination of words and images on film or video. These will give your speech another dimension. It is relatively simple to take a videocassette with you, if you are sure that there will be a videocassette recorder (VCR) and a television set available.

You can also use a video camera with a microcassette, but again be certain that your camera will connect with the television set available. Sometimes even state-of-the-art television sets just don't connect.

DISCOVER THE

VARIETY,

VERSATILITY,

AND

VALUE

OF

VISUALS

THE POWERFUL TOOL

Sight combined with sound is a powerful tool for a public speaker, so if there is an overhead projector available, learn to make the best use of it. With your visuals you can highlight points in your speech, present extra information, charts, artwork, emphasize particular elements, reinforce your ideas, and summarize.

DO-IT-YOURSELF

Visuals do not have to be professionally prepared. You can make your own transparencies. A drawing and/or words can be put on paper, then put through an ordinary photocopier onto special plain paper copier transparency film. The photocopier also allows you to edit, reduce or enlarge the original, as well as reproduce halftones or pictures. A color photocopier offers endless scope for your imagination.

If you have a computer, anything your computer can produce can be made into a transparency through your own printer, but here too you must have the correct transparency film. If you don't want to do your own, you can have transparencies made by an artist or an agency.

ONLY AN AID

No matter how artistic your visuals are, they are still only an aid. They must not dominate. Make sure they are appropriate for the occasion and can be seen from anywhere in the room. A complex visual is difficult to interpret.

Turn the projector light off between showing visuals so that your audience's attention returns to you, and never make the mistake of delivering your speech to the screen rather than to the people who have come to hear you.

SORTING OUT THE MASS OF
STATE-OF-THE-ART
EQUIPMENT

ADDING THAT TOUCH OF BRILLIANCE

If you want to go further than handling a basic overhead projector, you need to delve deeply because there is a mass of superb equipment on the market. The quality of color and clarity increases with the sophistication of the projector, including those that allow you to add multimedia to your presentation at the touch of a button. With some you don't have to stand beside your projector, you use a remote control as you move around the room.

COMPUTER FRIENDLY

There are projectors that can be linked with your personal computer, and some have a stereo audio output system. Some allow you to zoom in on specific information and reveal your message point by point, and automatically adjust brightness, contrast, and computer synchronization.

Among the many varieties available are easel pads, slide and desktop projectors, projection panels, and liquid crystal display panels. For audiovisuals there are videocassette players/recorders and motion picture projectors.

TAKE IT WITH YOU

You can also get projectors that connect with your VCR, laser disc player, speakers, or other multimedia equipment.

Some projectors are so compact and lightweight, they are ideal for carrying with you when you go to give a speech.

If you are a professional lecturer, you may consider having your own projector. This certainly saves the time and effort of checking out everyone else's equipment when you arrive at an engagement. But before you buy, get expert advice.

YOU'VE JUST BEEN TO A GREAT FUNCTION... SEMINAR... CONFERENCE...

YOU ENJOYED IT BECAUSE ...

- **E**VERYTHING WENT SMOOTHLY

- **T**HE SPEAKERS WERE OUTSTANDING

- **I**T RAN ON TIME

- **T**HE FOOD WAS DELICIOUS

HOW WAS IT DONE?

WRITE IT DOWN

It went smoothly because it was well organized. Next time you go to such an occasion make a note of all that went well—and all that did not. This gives you an excellent record of how a conference or seminar is planned. It's a good idea to have a notebook with you and jot down anything that you feel justifies mention.

Such an occasion demands a lot of preparation—weeks or even months of it. The final outcome shows you the degree of success that has been achieved.

QUESTIONS

Was there adequate parking? Were you greeted as you arrived? Did you have a comfortable seat? Could you see the platform easily? Was there easy access to the rest rooms? Was the room or hall large enough? Was it too large for the numbers attending? Was it over or underheated? Was the platform set up properly? What was the lighting like? Did the microphone work efficiently? Was there a lectern, and was it needed? Were speakers given a special place to sit during the conference?

NO MATTER HOW SMALL

How did the chairperson conduct the program? Was each speaker introduced competently? Were the speakers at ease in the surroundings? Could you hear them well? Did each speaker fit into the overall program with ease? Were there any breakdowns during the day?

Was there any handout material? Was it sufficient for your needs? Were there enough breaks in the program? Was the food of a high standard?

Make a note of even the smallest detail, for it is on these that many a function has foundered.

There can never be

a moment

when language

truly stands still,

any more than there is

a pause

in the ever-blazing

thoughts of men.

WILHELM VON HUMBOLDT

ON THE GO

What I love about language is that it is constantly changing. Once upon a time the change took place more slowly; people didn't move around a lot and they lived in small communities. In fact, until recent times, in a remote area in my homeland of Ireland, there were people who spoke close to Elizabethan English—and I do mean Elizabeth the first!

BLAME IT ON THE MEDIA

Today, with radio and television influencing every sector of society and with tourists traveling all over the world, our language is changing much more rapidly. Even dialects are fading a little, which is sad. But that is so-called progress.

The good side is that we are evolving into speakers who use language without the tight restrictions of earlier days. Listen to a recording of someone speaking even 30 years ago and you'll notice how old fashioned he or she sounds. They use written-style language, dated phraseology, and even the quality of their voices sounds unnatural, as if they were on their best behavior.

TRUE LEADERS

Unfortunately when some people speak in public today they resort to this style of speaking. But to the listener they sound rather like the recording—out-of-date.

If this is your problem, think of those "ever-blazing thoughts" and pay special attention to the true leaders of language, those who use it superbly. They can teach us all such a lot.

SCENARIO

You belong to a club that encourages good
speech and communication...or one that has
"service" as its aim...or promotes crafts...
or gardening...or whatever.

You have a guest speaker coming.
Perhaps you're having a competition and are
expecting a judge. Maybe your guest is someone
who holds an important position in your national
or international organization.

You've done a lot of preparation, but
the occasion doesn't go quite as well as
you had hoped. It's a little stilted, and
there has been some embarrassment.
Mistakes are made.

WHY?

What should have happened?

PREPARATION IS NOT ENOUGH

Don't get me wrong, preparation is vital. Without it everything can collapse. But on top of all the planning and organization there has to be a sense of expertise and style to carry the occasion through to a satisfying conclusion.

Every club should have at least one member—and preferably more—who has the ability to take over with authority and polish. She must greet guests with confidence, look after them with grace, and introduce them with skill.

FLOUNDERING

Too often guests are left wondering why they've come, when members flounder, are too shy to speak to them or are unsure what they should say if they do.

It is disconcerting for a guest to sit and watch an amateur speaker babble away on the platform and give an incoherent speech of welcome. It is embarrassing for them to feel like a fish out of water while the meeting goes through its motions with a seemingly endless agenda.

IRRITATION

The people in charge of the meeting must be authoritative in voice and body language. They must have the occasion so well organized that everyone knows what they are doing at every stage. Nothing irritates speakers more than to see members unsure of themselves, hesitating, muddling through, wasting their guests' precious time.

In fact, most speakers and judges prefer to arrive when the main business of the meeting is over. If they're invited to come earlier, that meeting should be planned to take as little time as possible.

YOU'VE BEEN ASKED TO GIVE A

SPEECH

DON'T BE FOOLED

A "thank you" speech seems so short and simple that you may not take it seriously. After all, what have you to do but stand up, say "thank you," and sit down again?

Don't be fooled! If you want to make this your debut into public speaking, regard this little speech as an adventure. Make it memorable. Plan it. Practice it.

NO CONFIDENCE

I once knew someone who was faced with such a speech. She hadn't done any public speaking before because she lacked confidence. However, the thank you speech was something she couldn't get out of, so she got started and made her grand plan.

To save herself from the embarrassment of making a fool of herself, she signed up for a few lessons in speech. These gave her a feeling for words, showed her how she could overcome her fear and speak up in public, and formed the basis of other possible speeches.

OUT THEY WENT

Next she wrote and rewrote her speech, constantly rehearsing it until she felt comfortable with her flow of language. She spoke it out loud in the shower and in the car. She began to discover how certain phrases flowed more easily than others. She realized, too, that some words were more difficult to pronounce when she was nervous, so out they went.

The result? A success that even she hadn't expected. Her short speech went extremely well. As a professional she had often been asked to give talks on her area of expertise but had always turned down the invitations. So the fact that she had laid the foundation for further speaking in public was important.

YOU'VE BEEN ASKED TO

MAKE A SPEECH AT A

WEDDING

CHAMPAGNE AND TOAST

There's nothing like a wedding to bring out the worst in a speaker. Whether it is the champagne or the exotic setting many speeches go on far too long and are embarrassing in their schmaltz—not to mention sexual innuendo.

The word *toast* is somewhat old fashioned today, but, call it what you will, at weddings or other ceremonies people still make speeches of celebration and congratulations.

NO SMUT

Speakers at these events are often coerced into taking part because they are family members or friends. Nervousness and alcohol, combined with inexperience and shyness, can make even a simple toast seem terrifying.

The easy way out is only to speak for as long as you feel comfortable. If that is just a few words—the toast itself—do it in a strong, clear voice and don't apologize. If you feel confident enough to add a little more, do so. If you can include a humorous anecdote or two, great, but keep it short, keep it tight, and, most important, keep it relatively clean. Guests in general do not like smut for smut's sake, neither do they appreciate long, rambling speeches.

WHO DOES WHAT

Once upon a time there used to be set rules for the toasts and who toasted whom. Now those rules have almost disappeared and each bridal couple has their own ideas. I have been to weddings with a few toasts and to others with many. Find out exactly what will be happening and plan your speech accordingly.

THE AFTER-DINNER SPEAKER

COMPETING WITH

THE FOOD

THE DRINK

THE TIME

AND THE TIREDNESS

NOT TO MENTION

THE NOISE

AND POSSIBLE

HECKLING

ON YOUR TOES

Facing an audience that has wined and dined for an hour or so before you speak presents special kinds of problems. Depending on the sophistication of the group, you could be up against anything from polite boredom to outright clatter and confusion.

As any experienced after-dinner speaker will tell you, your main function is to entertain. You are not there to instruct, to educate, to coach, or give a lecture. You are there to enliven the evening with a speech that is interesting, witty, and suitable for the occasion.

OUT WITH THE WORN OUT!

An entertaining after-dinner speech is easier if you share a common interest with your audience such as sports, real estate, or the financial market; but even here you must take care, as worn-out stories or quotations can irritate the audience.

It is also important to remember that although you want to entertain, you are not there as a comedian—unless you really are one. Stringing together a lot of dubious jokes is both boring and sometimes insulting to your audience.

THE NATURAL FLOW

Be funny if you can but don't make a fetish out of it. Humor can't be discovered in a book or played by rules—it's a natural flow of comedy that comes from within. Some people have the gift of making others laugh by the raise of an eyebrow or with a few simple words, but the rest of us are better off sticking to what we do best—perhaps relating an amusing incident or creating a humorous word picture.

SAME SPEECH

DIFFERENT
PLACES

YOUR SPEECH "WARDROBE"

It pays to have the basis of several speeches ready at all times. You never know when you are going to be called upon to give one.

A well-planned speech is rather like a cleverly planned wardrobe; those who look best always have a basic wardrobe of quality, tailored clothes that can be mixed and matched with a variety of other garments and colors. They are the ones who never complain, "I have nothing to wear."

VERSATILE

If you plan your speech wardrobe in the same way, you might be amazed how versatile it can be. Take a subject you know well. Prepare the basis of your first speech from it. List the main points: the angles you want to cover; descriptions; humor; and so on. Plot it on the moon chart (see pages 90–91).

Look at it from a variety of points of view. How could you adapt it to this audience or that? What would you have to add to make it more interesting? What might you have to leave out and what other material would be suitable to put in instead?

NO "QUICKIE"

When you have a speech on one subject ready to go at a ring of the telephone, move on to other subjects. Do research, plan carefully, have your basic speeches complete as far as information is concerned. The wardrobe mustn't become a quick, last-minute throw-together. It must have substance. It must have flair. In this way, the twist you give it for different audiences makes it come out fresh, as though you had just created it.

THE ULTIMATE COMPLIMENT

BEING INVITED TO
CHAIR A MEETING

POWER AND PURPOSE

Being asked to chair a meeting, whether it's at a corporate convention or a gathering of volunteers, is an honor. In every case the person in the chair (hereafter to be called "the chair") must have a very good grasp of the rules of procedure. It is the chair's job to control the meeting, to link the audience with the official side of the business, and to guide the meeting impartially.

FALLING SHORT

When a meeting falls short of expectations, the blame can usually be laid squarely at the chair's feet. A chair who allows a meeting to run overtime, who has no control over long-winded speakers, who dithers and is seen to be weak and easily swayed, should not have been given the task in the first place.

The best chairs I've seen in action are those who are in command even before the meetings begin. They are purposeful from the moment they arrive, have all the information prepared, and, most important, know how to handle the type of meeting it will be.

IN COMMAND

Business meetings have to be tightly controlled, and the chair must have a real understanding of their purpose and of the people attending. At public meetings the chair's influence often includes being a leader as well, so it is important to give each side a fair hearing, while still retaining command.

Social gatherings are more informal, where the chair also acts as host. Yet even in these situations an efficient chair can make the sessions more enjoyable.

BEING INTERVIEWED
ON THE RADIO

(OVER  THE TELEPHONE?)

AN UNSEEN AUDIENCE

Public speaking does not always mean facing an audience. If you are being interviewed, giving a talk, or taking part in a discussion on radio, your audience will be vast, but no one will see you. They will only hear your voice.

How your voice sounds will influence listeners almost as much as what you say, so speak clearly, keep it lively, and don't babble. Of course you will be nervous, but you must control it. A microphone is very sensitive and picks up sounds that would otherwise not be heard.

DID I SAY THAT?!

If your radio interview or program is recorded in a studio, mistakes can be edited out, but with a live broadcast what you say is what the listeners will hear.

Many radio station personalities conduct interviews over the telephone during live broadcasts. A time will be set up and the call will come through on the dot. You must be ready to answer questions, even though you probably won't have any idea what the interviewer will ask you.

JUST A CHAT

Some of these telephone interviews are for news sessions and will be short—a minute or two perhaps—and to the point, so don't chatter on. Others are longer and more informal. This gives you an opportunity to expand and discuss your subject in greater detail. Forget that you're on the radio and talk in a relaxed way as though to a friend.

If you are pushed into a hostile situation, it is important that you keep calm. A hasty or angry answer could damage your public image.

THE TESTING TIME

APPEARING ON
TELEVISION

TELEVISIONITIS

Nothing can terrify a speaker more than the thought of appearing in front of not hundreds but millions of people. Television can be a most penetrating medium, but sometimes a trivial one. You are seen close up, but may only have minutes or even seconds to put your point across, yet your performance could change people's opinions of you.

BACK TO BASICS

Basic principles apply. Be natural and honest. Don't try any cover-up—audiences hate deception. In just a minute they will judge you as someone with authority, intelligence, humor, and common sense—or the opposite!

Whether you are part of an in-depth program or a short one, if it is done in a studio, you are out of your own environment. You have to compensate for this by controlling your fears and emotions and keeping your head clear to understand and answer the questions put to you.

The thought of appearing on television is more daunting than actually doing it. Regard it as a challenge. Take care to dress appropriately and be well groomed. Deep breathing helps to calm the nerves, but avoid alcohol. Remember to smile—unless you are involved in a disaster—but don't look at the camera unless you're told to.

Although there will be a lot of people around you in the studio, try not to get distracted. Imagine yourself being alone with the interviewer, but talking to someone you love who is watching from her living room and thinking how well you're doing.

If the cameras come to you, the situation is different. You are on your ground and will feel more confident, but the same rules apply.

THE PRESS RELEASE

HOW TO...
TO WHOM...
WHY...
WHAT...
WHERE...

FROM EAR TO EYE

The mistake some people make is that (a) they prepare their spoken speech in written form suitable for being read, or (b) they hand the press a copy of a speech designed for being heard. There is a distinct difference.

The written speech you take with you onto the platform must be exactly as you will say it. It should have the easy flow of colloquial speech complete with contractions such as *I'm, we'll, can't,* and *won't.* It must not have the more formal structure of words that are read.

SLOPPY

If you hand the press a copy of your speech with its seemingly sloppy (to the eye) writing they may not print it. Or, if they do, they might edit it, and this could change the meaning.

If you have to supply a copy for publication of any kind it is important to respect the difference between the spoken and the written word.

When you prepare your speech for the ear you say it out loud, over and over again. In the same way, when you write it for a press release, you must read it over and over again to make sure it makes sense and appeals to the eye.

INVITING THE PRESS

If you invite the press to attend, ensure that what you are going to say will be of value to their readers. It is irritating for a reporter to attend a session to find that it is on a specific subject that is of no interest to him or his readers.

If no one comes, send a copy of your release to the editor or reporter and hope that they may use even a paragraph from it. If they don't, forget it. It is exasperating for an editor to receive a truculent call from a contributor who has been turned down. That could work against you next time.

After a FAILURE

HOW DO YOU GET YOUR CONFIDENCE BACK?

PICKING YOURSELF UP

We are all delicate beings and it doesn't take much to bruise our egos, especially when we're new to the game of public speaking. The danger lies in not picking ourselves up and starting again soon. Many a fine speaker has been lost because of an ingrained fear of open spaces and frowning faces.

TOUGH NUT

Ask yourself why you failed. Was it lack of preparation? Perhaps it was an inability to remember what you wanted to say or read what you had written? Was it plain nervousness? Or a combination of these things? It was probably the latter.

There is no surefire way to overcome nervousness, but it is surprising what you can do by discovering that tough little nut inside you. Once the bruising has disappeared, make yourself speak up. Start small if you prefer. A short speech—one or two minutes perhaps—done well can ease the pain of failure. But whatever you do, make sure you are thoroughly prepared. Rehearse it again and again.

THINK SUCCESS

Don't be afraid to admit a past failure. You may be surprised to discover that every other person you know has had the same experience. Talk it over. You'll get help, advice, and, most importantly, support. This support does wonders for your confidence.

Always remember that if you think failure, failure is what you'll get. This is almost always the case when you're speaking in public. Train yourself to think positively. Think success. That's what all the speakers you admire do.

FAILURE

is instructive.
The person who really
thinks learns quite as
much from his failures
as from his successes.

JOHN DEWEY

END OF THE WORLD?

This is a favorite maxim of mine! I keep saying that you mustn't treat a failure as a disaster, so it is extremely satisfying to know that the same theory came from such an illustrious person as John Dewey—professor, philosopher, psychologist, educator, and one of the founders of the Philosophical School of Pragmatism.

SO WHAT?

What he said should be part of everyone's thinking. If you make a mistake, so what? It's not the end of the world.

I meet people who have failed when speaking in public and to them it's like a great wall that they can't climb back over. They're afraid to try again or if they do they do it with fear in their hearts and clamps on their tongues.

THE PERSON WHO THINKS

What I like about this quotation is the phrase, "The person who really thinks..." This could be the key to success. *Thinking* means that you work through the emotion, the humiliation, the fear, and the anxiety. You analyze the reasons why you failed—lack of preparation, lack of confidence, lack of the right word at the right time.

When the thinking pays off and you know yourself better, try again. Start small. Put as much work into a half-minute speech or mini talk as you would with a much longer one. Keep telling yourself that this time you'll be a success.

Then give it all you've got, and sit back and bask in your success. Think of it as the key to your regeneration!

WHEN ENGLISH
IS YOUR SECOND LANGUAGE

GLüCKWüNSCHE

秋

WHAT ARE YOUR CHANCES
OF SUCCESS?

le mere du Sud

大

美

品

Dobrai Ootrah

HELP IS AT HAND

If you are reasonably fluent in English there is nothing to stop you from becoming a public speaker. However, there are some obvious rules that must be obeyed. The way you speak the language has to be clear enough for people to understand you. If you have difficulty pronouncing words, it is essential to get help. A friend who speaks English well could demonstrate how the words should be said, but if you want to really succeed, a course with a qualified speech teacher would be better.

CONCENTRATION

It is extremely important that you gain an understanding of how words are spoken in phrases and sentences. If they come out in a monotonous or convoluted way, your audience will find it difficult to concentrate, especially since they must cope with your accent as well. A microphone can make it harder, so don't speak too quickly.

Your speech has to be lively and full of vitality with constant changes of pitch and pace. It must also be presented in such a way that an English-speaking audience can follow your reasoning.

KEEP IT SIMPLE

It is best to start with a simple theme, simply spoken. This will help you to gain the confidence needed to go further into the field of public speaking. So often speakers from different cultures have an incredible store of knowledge and experience to impart, but are hampered by their delivery. Learn to speak in "word pictures" (see *The Power of Speech*). This will help you talk to your audience in a way that they will really enjoy, as well as interpret correctly.

TRICKS OF SPEECH

21 ways

to make

what you say

memorable

SOUNDING DIFFERENT

You don't want to sound like an inexperienced speaker, so here are a few reminders to help lift your performance and acceptance by your audience. None of them are really difficult. They just need to be practiced.

1. Simplify your language—from words to sentences and phrases.

2. Never use written-style language.

3. Dump euphemisms; phrases like "little girls' room" sound silly.

4. Avoid jargon.

5. Too many negatives can be so depressing.

6. Use active verbs and phrases, not passive ones.

7. Include the personal touch—audiences like to know how you feel.

8. Throw out words that are tongue twisters or they'll trip you up.

9. Repetition occasionally has power. It adds strength.

10. Only tell a joke if you're sure you can tell it well.

11. Never swear—except when you're certain it will be accepted!

12. Chop the heads off clichés. Who needs overworked phrases?

13. To hold your audience, change your pitch and pace constantly.

14. Remember the power of the pause. Never substitute "ums" and "ers."

15. Put color into your language. This adds life and vitality.

16. Keep warmth in your voice to show people that you care.

17. Use vivid imagery to highlight your words and your meaning.

18. Don't talk in contractions—many listeners will not understand.

19. Keep your speech rhythmic and unpredictable.

20. Use a variety of adjectives—"wonderful" all the time gets boring.

21. And finally, the best advice of all: Speak from the heart.

ARS EST
CELARE
ARTEM